Beyond Friendship

The Future of Anglo–American Relations

Heritage
$4.95

Beyond Friendship

The Future of Anglo–American Relations

Robin Harris

214 Massachusetts Avenue, NE
Washington, DC 20002–4999
(202) 546-4400 • heritage.org
ThatcherCenter.org

Printed in the United States of America.

ISBN: 0-89195-273-x

Contents

ooooo

Introduction

THE PURPOSE OF THIS BOOK is to look forward to the future, but the reader will quickly observe that about half of it relates to the past. I make no apology for this. The "Special Relationship" between the United Kingdom and the United States—which I shall argue does truly exist, ought to exist, and should be made still stronger—is rooted in the two nations' history. It cannot properly be understood outside that context.

To recognize this is not to be nostalgic: It is to be realistic. British Prime Minister Tony Blair's favorite touchstone for policymaking is "what works." Within limits, it is a good one. The Special Relationship can indeed be shown to "work," though not always. In assessing the conditions under which it flourishes and under which it withers, we must examine the triumphs and tribulations, and even the banalities of its trouble-free existence, from the past.

On the other hand, history does not teach everything we need to know about the future.

Adapting to global changes, using them, not misreading or falling foul of them will be a major challenge for the leaders of Britain and America over many decades to come. In doing this, good personal relationships, though useful, will not be enough.

Indeed, it is the argument of this book that somewhat too much time and energy has been invested in dressing up what is essentially a close alliance in the garb of a slightly corny romantic friendship. It is by understanding the two countries' national interests, addressing public concerns about them, and then cementing those interests still more closely together that the Special Relationship will be made to hold.

Robin Harris
May 2006

○○○○○

Executive Summary

The Anglo-American Special Relationship is of great mutual benefit to both parties and should be strengthened. The United States has in Britain its only militarily effective and politically reliable global ally—a fact confirmed by past attempts to find an alternative. The Special Relationship with Britain does not complicate, but rather supports, America's operation as a global superpower. The U.K. gains even more. Its economy gets a boost; its interests are protected; its security is increased (through vital intelligence sharing); and its standing in the world is immeasurably enhanced.

The Special Relationship's history provides clues to how it can be made to work better today. The expression, coined by Winston Churchill, was never intended as an exercise in nostalgia, though the common experience of the two nations does makes it unique. It implied close practical collaboration in security and military affairs, and this is how it must finally be judged.

The Relationship depends in part upon good personal relations between American Presidents and British Prime Ministers, as when Harold Macmillan intervened with John F. Kennedy to secure Polaris against the doubts of the U.S. State Department and Pentagon. Warm personal relations and mutual political understanding between Margaret Thatcher and Ronald Reagan were even more important in the 1980s. The Reagan Administration's support for Britain in the Falklands and Mrs. Thatcher's support for America in the Libyan raid were moments when the Relationship could have fractured if the wrong decisions had been taken.

But the Anglo–American Relationship worked, in the last analysis, primarily because of the two nations' shared goals, above all the defeat of Soviet communism. And at no stage did either Margaret Thatcher or Ronald Reagan forget their own countries' national interests.

Tony Blair was right to invest so much effort in repairing the Special Relationship when he came to power, initially with President Bill

Clinton. He was also correct, and his many domestic critics were wrong, when he strongly supported President George W. Bush in the wake of 9/11 in Afghanistan and then in Iraq. Yet the terms on which he felt he had to do so and the means he employed have, unfortunately, put the foundations of the Relationship at risk.

As a utopian liberal internationalist, Blair could not publicly support America's objectives and rhetoric, instead concentrating his justification for war on WMD rather than espousing regime change as such. He similarly refused to abandon his commitment to close relations with "Old Europe," continuing to deny the reality of deep-rooted European hostility to the U.S., its policies, and its allies. Worse, he never explained in a frank manner to the British public why it was in Britain's national interest to support America.

The Special Relationship between the U.S. and the U.K. thus seemed simply a friendship between the American and British leaders, in which the latter lacked any significant influence. As a result, public and political opinion in Britain is now worryingly anti-American. This is particularly important because, unless reversed, distrust of America may prevent British involvement in or even support for further action against rogue states and terrorist regimes.

Moreover, through continuing European integration, especially in defense, Britain under Blair has been sucked further into arrangements which will render it difficult for the British to remain the reliable ally they have so often proved to be. An important element of this is defense procurement. Regrettably, the Bush Administration continues to support European integration, even endorsing the now rejected European Constitution. If the Special Relationship is to survive, let alone fulfil its potential, a different approach in a range of areas will be needed in the post-Blair era.

The fundamental change needed is open and honest recognition by both parties that the U.K.–U.S. Relationship is a reflection of real national interests, not a corny friendship between equals. The U.S. should be clear in what it expects from, and reliable in what it offers to, Britain. This means, on the one hand, taking Britain into its confidence and listening to British representations in a systematic manner. If

British troops are to be deployed in support of U.S. policy, Britain must feel a part of it—without, of course, being allowed a veto. If Britain is a special military partner, it should be granted special privileges in defense procurement and elsewhere.

The U.S. also needs to clarify its attitude toward the emerging European megastate, which is a competitor and not a reliable collaborator. Far from persuading Britain to integrate further, the U.S. should be urging U.K. disengagement, particularly in the military field.

On the other hand, the U.S. should be less reticent about British shortcomings. It should insist that Britain support U.S. goals in different regions and forums rather than try to play to other galleries. It should also press the British government to take vigorous action against Islamic extremism, which has been allowed to gain a grip on British cities.

Similarly, America should no longer be prepared to accept at face value Britain's defense effort. Although the U.K. has superb fighting troops, its defense budget has shrunk while Blair's internationalism has increased deployments.

In the longer term, America needs to put much greater effort into its public diplomacy focused on Britain. The anti-Americanism that is now prevalent in the British electronic media receives no effective response. The U.S. also should be much less complacent about the growing divergence between the two countries' cultural, social, and economic models. Although not easy to influence, these trends, if they continue, are likely to lead to political divergence as well.

As for Britain, its government must be seen to defend the national interest in its dealing with the U.S. The Special Relationship should not prevent that; but Britain will also have to make sacrifices to retain its influence in Washington, including the loss of British lives, both military and civilian, in support of U.S. goals. This can be spelled out realistically to the British people, who are quite up to coping with both war and terrorism. If the Anglo–American Special Relationship is once again understood as more than friendship, it will be stronger—and so, paradoxically, will the friendship.

ooooo I ooooo

How Special a Relationship?

Grounds for Confidence

The most distinguished and enthusiastic current proponent of the Special Relationship between the United States and Britain is undoubtedly former Prime Minister Margaret Thatcher. This, of course, is enough to turn some fastidious souls off the whole idea; but her views are important, not least because she achieved, by the common consent of supporters and critics alike, a uniquely close and effective bond with her opposite number in the White House, Ronald Reagan. Exactly why this political and personal friendship worked so well, and how it worked, will be examined separately,[1] but the power of its impact is indisputable.

[1] Lady Thatcher has given her own account in *The*

Moreover, Lady Thatcher has also given her reflections in some detail upon why the Relationship mattered in her day and will continue to matter. She stresses the commonality of outlook of the two countries which is rooted in their history—and not just modern history, but the collective experience which preceded the American Revolution and political separation. In short, the two nations share common values—and not any old values. These particular values are quite distinctive and explain both the Anglo–Saxon political, social, and economic model's success and its creative applicability to the modern world. They also now make America supremely well-equipped for world leadership.

Because America's commitment to liberty is so bound up with the American nation's conception of its very identity, American power poses no threat to the liberty of other nations. For this reason, among others related to capacity, stability, and security, Lady Thatcher therefore welcomes the global pre-eminence

Downing Street Years (London: HarperCollins, 1993), pp. 156–171, 244–248, 463–473, and 768–777.

of the American superpower. Any worries she has about America's actions are likely to stem either from a feeling that the U.S. Administration may at any particular time have misread the situation or from a deeper anxiety that the United States may be surrendering excessive influence to other powers which should not be entrusted with it. Without believing in an enforceable *Pax Americana*, she passionately believes that without *Potestas Americana*, there will be no *Pax* worth its salt.

Not even all Americans would agree with this analysis. Many American liberals seem to feel, rather as successive Federal Chancellors of (West) Germany have felt, that their own country's power is already so great that it needs to be constrained—in the American instance, by the United Nations; in Germany's, by a federal Europe. Among American conservatives, there are also divisions about how widespread and how permanent America's international responsibilities should be. But whatever the nuances and language, the Thatcher view is certainly very close to that which currently prevails in Washington regarding the exertion of American power. It also constitutes the most coherent and optimistic view of America's leadership to be found on the British side of the Atlantic.[2]

Coherence and optimism are not, indeed, the obvious qualities that spring to mind when one considers the attitudes of most of the British foreign policy establishment. This is reflected in its representatives' views of the Anglo–American relationship.

British Doubts

In his rather misleadingly entitled memoirs, *DC Confidential*, Britain's most recent ambassador to the United States, Sir Christopher Meyer, recalls some instructions which he gave on arrival in Washington:

> I would not allow the phrase "special relationship" inside the embassy. I was worried that my staff would approach their work with a set of delusions: that Britain's relations with the US were different in kind from those with any

[2] Margaret Thatcher, *Statecraft: Strategies for a Changing World* (London: HarperCollins, 2002), pp. 19–62.

> other country; that the Americans would therefore grant us special benefits, unavailable to other nations; and that as a result, developing a relationship with the US of advantage to Britain would require less effort than with other governments….
>
> A phrase like this…merits use only to describe those very few relationships where a foreign government has the ability significantly to influence US politics and, through this, the direction of US foreign policy. Only Israel, Taiwan, Saudi Arabia and the Irish Republic have shown this quality consistently over the years.[3]

This observation, as one would expect from a talented graduate of the British Foreign Office school of statecraft, contains a mixture of shrewd insight and perverse wrongheadedness. As the ambassador himself often saw, despite

---

[3] Christopher Meyer, *DC Confidential* (London: Weidenfeld and Nicolson, 2005), pp. 56–57.

attempts by Number Ten Downing Street to exclude him from some aspects of it, the Special Relationship was very close indeed during all of his time in Washington—even *too* close, some critics would argue. But, that said, his qualifications have some force. Naturally, British diplomats would be foolish to bank on favors when it comes to advancing British interests in America. Naturally, too, a great power—indeed, a global superpower—like the United States has to maintain a range of international relationships which are in various fashions and degrees special.

One could, in fact, quarrel with Sir Christopher's preferred list, which lumps together very different international ties. The U.S.–Irish link, for example, is almost entirely sentimental. By contrast, no sentiment at all (indeed, an increasing degree of suspicion) characterizes U.S. ties with Saudi Arabia, whose significance is almost wholly determined by Saudi oil reserves. Taiwan is again in a quite different category. It has not, in fact, in the past managed to lobby particularly effectively; hence the collapse of the old "Two China" policy under Richard Nixon. It now features large in U.S. calculations because it has a huge, predatory neighbor in the form of the People's Republic of China, which, as President George W. Bush rightly stated to much diplomatic distress, is America's "strategic competitor."

Israel has a particular place apart in the list. American–Israeli relations are truly "special" in something of the sense in which Anglo–American relations are "special." American commitment to Israel's survival and security is absolute. One could imagine Washington, *in extremis*, abandoning any ordinary ally but never withdrawing protection from Tel Aviv. Initially, this too was a matter of sentiment. Today, Israel also serves—and indeed has served ever since the Seven Day War—as an effective American ally of military significance in a region where the U.S. has few friends. In the event of the crisis with Iran reaching the point at which military action is required, Israel may even be called upon to act as an American military surrogate. But Israel is necessarily a regional rather than a global force. It is, in the last resort, too small and too vulnerable to do more than repay something of the commitment which the United States makes to it while, of course, putting its own national interest first.

There are also candidates for "special relationship" status which have at least as much right to inclusion on the list as some of Meyer's nominees. For example, the alliance with Japan is fundamental to American interests and to stability in Asia. And what of Australia, an increasingly significant regional power, which under Prime Minister John Howard's leadership openly affirms that the relationship with America is "the most important we have with any single country" and actually sends troops in to prove it?[4] Last (and definitely least), even Mexico was at one time considered ripe for a special relationship status—an illusion which soon melted into the sands of traditional Latino vs. Gringo hostility.

American Doubts

Lying behind the reluctance of Britain's diplomats and politicians to use the term "special relationship" is also something less palatable. It is the awareness that a certain strand of American opinion finds the concept empty

---

[4] See Rupert Darwall, "John Howard's Australia," *Policy Review*, August/September 2005, p. 61.

or even ludicrous. President Bill Clinton, in preparing for his first meeting with his British opposite number, Prime Minister John Major, was reminded to mention the magic phrase. "Oh yes," said Clinton. "How could I forget?" At which he burst out laughing.[5]

Many people, not least in Britain, have subsequently laughed at John Major, and the newly elected President had no reason to feel well-disposed toward him, since Conservative Party officials had become imprudently involved in the failed Bush campaign. The Clinton White House would, in any case, adopt a different tack in relations with Britain once Tony Blair became Prime Minister in 1997. Yet the initial mockery reflected more than mere pique, or even Clinton's trademark cynicism. It reflected continuing doubts which regularly surface as each new Administration seeks to review America's broader policy options.

American doubts about the Relationship do not, at least in recent times, spring from hostility to Britain as such. Once, with a little

[5] Raymond Setz, *Over Here* (London: Phoenix, 1998), p. 322.

American help, the United Kingdom was no longer an imperial power and, once again with American participation, British attempts to pursue an independent policy in the Middle East were destroyed by Suez, there were no more serious grounds for rivalry. The United States held the floor as the undisputed Anglo-Saxon superpower. Britain had been relegated militarily to the second division, with its poor economic performance and its elite's self-doubts doing the rest. Indeed, throughout the 1960s and 1970s, the U.S. was more likely to be worried about Britain's weakness than concerned that she might cause America trouble; and when, in the 1980s, Britain did revive, it was under a British government that was resolutely pro-American.

The doubts, then, have stemmed from something quite different: America's continuing and understandable desire to re-prioritize its relationships to reflect changing global realities. Hence the talk in the 1990s of the United States looking westward to the Pacific, where the most vibrant economies were to be found. Hence, too, the thinking behind a revived hemispheric policy to unite Latin American countries, starting with Mexico, with the United States in a free trade zone of stability and democracy. Neither of these preoccupations has, in the event, proved particularly fruitful. As for the Pacific, China continues to dominate—and to threaten—East Asia. As for Latin America, U.S. relations with Mexico are uncertain, and there is now hardly a government in South America which is not more or less hostile to American interests.

However, the most important focus for these regular policy reappraisals by the U.S. has, over the decades, been Europe, where some in the State Department hoped and expected that an alternative to Britain as a partner would emerge. This was never, of course, likely to be France, with or without Charles de Gaulle. Germany was always more suitable culturally and temperamentally, but obviously it could not play any such role while divided. However, as soon as the Iron Curtain was torn down, the United States hastened to offer precisely this opportunity to Chancellor Helmut Kohl, who now presided over the richest and most populous country in Europe. President George H. W. Bush thus told the Germans when he visited Mainz at the end of May 1989 that they could become "partners in leadership," something which not even the Special Relationship implied.

This improbable partnership, in practice, came to nothing, and no one, even in deference to current Chancellor Angela Merkel, is likely to suggest its re-creation. If not Germany, and in the absence of any other suitable European power, the only alternative to Britain on offer was an entirely new megastate—the European Union. But that too has its problems, as will be discussed in the context of current challenges.

The fact that other avenues, particularly other European avenues, have proved disappointing for American foreign-policy makers is, however, in itself no proof of the worth of the Special Relationship. A global superpower, the only pole in a unipolar world, the United States is not compelled to enter into enduring relationships with any state. It has to perceive interests that are satisfied by doing so. Nor should those in Britain who urge the Special Relationship's importance engage in special pleading based upon nostalgia for past comradeship, not least because the original case for the Relationship was based upon harsh reality, not comforting illusion.

Origins

It was, of course, Winston Churchill, in his famous 1946 "Sinews of Peace" address in Fulton, Missouri, who gave authoritative formulation to the concept. He spoke of shared democratic values, ones which he urged should be exported globally and which he presciently and controversially saw as threatened by the ambitions of Soviet communism, and he defined these values, as would Margaret Thatcher half a century later, as deriving from a continuous tradition of Anglo–American liberty. So he urged:

> We must never cease to proclaim in fearless tones the great principles of freedom and the rights of man which are the joint inheritance of the English-speaking world and which through Magna Carta, the Bill of Rights, the Habeas Corpus, trial by jury, and the English common law find their most

> famous expression in the American Declaration of Independence.[6]

Churchill assumed that Britain and America, whatever their particular national interests, were also the two nations where liberty was most secure and which could thus, in the final analysis, be best guaranteed to fight to defend it. History at this point touched directly upon strategies for security, and he made it clear that the latter were his central concern—"the crux," as he put it, of his message:

> Neither the prevention of war, nor the continuous rise of world organisation [i.e., the United Nations] will be gained without what I have called the fraternal association of the English-speaking peoples. This means a special relationship between the British Commonwealth and Empire and

[6] Winston Churchill, "Sinews of Peace," speech delivered at Westminster College, Fulton, Missouri, March 5, 1946, at *www.winstonchurchill.org/i4a/pages/index.cfm?pageid=429*.

> the United States. This is no time for generalities, and I will venture to be precise. Fraternal association requires not only the growing friendship and mutual understanding between our two vast but kindred systems of society, but the continuance of the intimate relationship between our military advisers, leading to common study of potential dangers, the similarity of weapons and manuals of instructions, and to the interchange of officers and cadets at technical colleges. It should carry with it the continuance of the present facilities for mutual security by the joint use of all Naval and Air Force bases in the possession of either country all over the world....[7]

One should note *en passant* that Churchill's conception of such a Special Relationship had no obvious precedents. No such thing, for example, was envisaged by Woodrow Wilson and

[7] *Ibid.*

Lloyd George. But the passage is also of significance for two very contemporary reasons.

First, Churchill makes clear that the Anglo–U.S. "fraternal association," which is intended to include the rest of the English-speaking world ("Commonwealth and Empire"), was to be a force for global peace and, indeed, serve as a fulcrum for wider international cooperation through the United Nations.

Second, the Special Relationship should not be a matter of "generalities" (as he put it), but rather would be embodied in the closest possible defense cooperation, stretching from the use of bases through weapons procurement and to everyday matters of training.

One should also, however, recall both the context and the aftermath of Fulton. Churchill's central theme, and the one which drew the most attention and much criticism, was his warning of an "Iron Curtain" which had "descended across the [European] Continent." The background to his plea for closer military collaboration was, therefore, acute military danger. The plea was in fact rejected, at least for the moment. Most Americans thought it alarmist (though not all policymakers—George Kennan's "Long

Telegram" had, after all, been sent the previous month). British press reaction was also mixed.

Yet Churchill was right. He was sometimes accused in the course of his long career of being a dreamer; but in the matter of the Anglo–American Special Relationship, he was highly practical. This Relationship, as he conceived it, was not at all to be a mere cultural artifact. It was to be a powerful and effective alliance, a continuation of a system tried and tested in war but now focused on a different threat: that from an aggressive and expansionist Soviet Union.

ooooo 2 ooooo

Perspectives on the Past

THERE IS ALWAYS A RISK, when reviewing the Special Relationship, that one may consider its origins and then its present operation (under President George W. Bush and Prime Minister Tony Blair) without also forming conclusions on the basis of what lies between. But the various crises and successes of those five decades do, in fact, have many lessons to teach. In particular, it is possible to assess how important at different times were three cardinal elements of the Relationship: personal relations between leaders, enduring national interest, and external threats. Any such assessment certainly reveals that no single one of these elements can provide a complete explanation of events.

For example, one might have expected that leaders who shared a similar political outlook would cooperate more effectively than those who did not.[1] This was by no means always so. The Conservative Leader Anthony Eden and the Republican President Dwight D. Eisenhower managed between them to plunge Anglo–American relations into unparalleled crisis at Suez. It was then a Conservative Prime Minister, Harold Macmillan, and a Democrat President, John F. Kennedy, who re-launched cooperation between the two countries. By contrast, the Labour Prime Minister, Harold Wilson, had a tense and unfriendly relationship with Kennedy's Democrat successor, Lyndon B. Johnson.

When Edward Heath's Conservative Party won the British general election in 1970, the Republican President Richard Nixon automatically assumed that Heath was a man with whom he could do business, but he was sharply, rudely, and repeatedly disillusioned. Heath snubbed all attempts to make the U.S.–U.K. Relationship "special" because he was determined to prove

[1] By contrast, similarities of values, in particular conservative values, rather than party political allegiance may well—as I shall argue—be an important underpinning of the Special Relationship.

Britain's European credentials to France—and also, no doubt, because ungraciousness came naturally to him. When the Americans—who, of course, had been pressing Britain closer to Europe for years—helpfully declared 1973 to be the "Year of Europe," this flattering gesture was merely deemed by Heath and his fellow European leaders to be unseemly meddling. And if the Heath and Nixon governments made many of the same mistakes in domestic policy—monetary indiscipline, overspending, price controls—it certainly never induced a common view on world affairs, let alone a sympathetic regard between the two leaders.[2]

It is less easy to point to occasions when the Special Relationship functioned well *despite* the pressures of national interests and external circumstances and merely *because of* personal or political closeness between leaders. Perhaps the nearest example is the warm relations enjoyed by President George H. W. Bush and British Prime Minister John Major—relations which

---

[2] See the account by Henry Kissinger, *Years of Renewal* (New York: Simon and Schuster, 1999), pp. 599–603.

apparently still continue. But it is difficult to attribute the success (though it is possible to attribute the shortcomings) of the first Gulf War to that close relationship,[3] and it is impossible to point to any other example of useful collaboration which subsequently flowed from it.

This, in itself, is significant. The actions of powers are always better predicted by the traditional assumptions of *Realpolitik* than they are by any others. If that was true in an age before democratic elections and an alert media presence, it is even truer now that decisions are so systematically scrutinized. Personal diplomacy taken to the extreme is the prerogative of princes, not politicians. Unfortunately, it tickles political vanity sometimes to forget that.

A variation on this theme is that what a country sacrifices for another is more significant

[3] Bush's and Major's lack of resolve allowed Saddam to survive and cause another war, just as their much-lauded pragmatism induced both to pledge low taxes and then raise them. They also pursued a disastrous policy in the Balkans which worked to the advantage of the aggressor, Serbia. And, of course, they both then lost elections. Personal sympathy between leaders is thus no substitute for getting agreed policies right.

than what a leader says to another. One can point, for example, to the contrast between the levels of influence wielded in Washington by two post–World War II British Labour Prime Ministers, Clement Attlee and Harold Wilson. Attlee was able to obtain a hearing from President Harry Truman, including a crucial assurance on the mooted use of the atomic weapon, because British troops were fighting alongside those of the United States in Korea at the time.[4] Wilson, though, had no significant influence over American policy under Johnson because—for good reasons—he refused to send British troops to Vietnam. Commitments of blood and treasure always, in the end, speak louder than words.

This is something which those who criticize Tony Blair's willingness to commit British troops in Iraq should remember. A general expression of support, even formal support in the U.N. Security Council, would have provided

[4] Attlee received an oral assurance that there would be no use of the atomic weapon in Korea without prior consultation with Britain, but Truman would not give a written one. David McCullough, *Truman* (New York: Simon and Schuster, 1992), pp. 825–826.

nothing like the leverage that military engagement made available to London. Whether Blair used that leverage wisely (or even at all) is, of course, a different matter, which will be addressed separately.

Personal and political closeness between leaders is therefore most important when it supplements the perceived interests of the two countries. Good personal relations have indeed often oiled the wheels of official diplomacy. They have allowed secondary or short-term obstacles to be overcome. They have also accelerated decisions, which the coldly calculated pursuit of national advantage would probably in the end have produced anyway—and so rendered those decisions more timely, unambiguous, and effective. On this, witness the Kennedy–Macmillan and Reagan–Thatcher relationships examined in more detail below.

A rarely discussed instance of the opposite is also worth mentioning: This is the relationship between Thatcher and President Jimmy Carter. It was not that the two got on badly, although Carter preferred dealing with Thatcher's Labour predecessor James Callaghan. And it should not be forgotten that it was the Carter

Administration that originally made the strategically crucial decision to supply Britain with the Trident I (C4) missile to update the British nuclear deterrent.

The fact remains, however, that if the two leaders had got on better personally, if they had established a surer bond of trust and sympathy, the immediate response to the Soviet invasion of Afghanistan in December 1979, which opened a new phase of the Cold War, would have been more formidable. Carter and Thatcher both agreed, of course, that the Soviet Union now had to be faced down, but Carter had so many of his own words to eat that it was difficult to articulate anything else. Had not Ronald Reagan been elected at this juncture, the confrontation with the Soviets would never have been so dramatic, intense, and successful as he and Margaret Thatcher made it.

A closer look at two specific phases of the Special Relationship will permit more detailed examination of the interplay of these different factors. Each, in its way, can be seen as a case study. The first, which concerns the first phase of post-war U.S.–U.K. nuclear cooperation, is essentially a study in crisis resolution.

The second, which concerns the unique Reagan–Thatcher partnership, is—despite the occasional misunderstandings and conflicts—a study in triumph.

Case Study #1: Nuclear and Political Fission (1945–1962)

Churchill's already quoted Fulton speech came at a particularly awkward time for Anglo–U.S. relations in one respect: cooperation (or, more precisely, non-cooperation) on the atomic weapon. British scientists had contributed significantly to the Manhattan Project and to the development of the weapons used against Japan; but with victory secured, Washington had no intention of sharing its expertise with Britain. The formal manifestation of this new attitude was the passing by Congress of the McMahon Act, which prohibited the exchange of atomic information between the U.S. and any other nation.

By slamming the door on Anglo–U.S. cooperation, the McMahon Act inadvertently encouraged Britain to go ahead with plans for its own independent deterrent. In retrospect, this was no bad thing. It proved—and was intended to prove—to the Americans that Britain was serious about remaining a major military power. But it was only the first of several shocks which such unilateral American decisions administered.

The two countries continued to go their separate ways on atomic energy matters, though this did not prevent military cooperation of other kinds in response to the more obvious and pressing Soviet threat. The British and American chiefs of staff, always keener on close relations than the politicians, kept in contact. Then Britain's role in the 1948 Berlin airlift demonstrated the country's worth as an effective ally to an otherwise skeptical U.S. State Department. In 1949, the Soviets tested their nuclear weapon. As tension grew in Europe, Britain's importance as an advance platform for the U.S. military grew. The stationing of American B-29 bombers in Britain meant that the country was now a potential target for Soviet attack in the case of hostilities. Inexorably, events were thus forcing the old wartime allies back together.

The establishment of NATO in 1949 is rightly regarded as a vital step toward securing eventual victory in the Cold War; but at a certain level, it also provided a complication for the Special Relationship. On the one hand, the U.S. regarded the relationship with Britain as, in Truman's words, "the mainspring of Atlantic Defense" (and not just Atlantic, given British commitments side by side with America in Korea). At the same time, however, the United States was also keen to emphasize the Western European dimension to the Cold War struggle. Too exclusive a commitment to Britain might render less credible America's wider plans for European self-defense. So the U.S. strongly backed the abortive European Defense Community, which Britain refused to join. This refusal provoked thinly veiled American threats to discontinue the Special Relationship.

The Suez crisis of 1956—for which both sides, in retrospect and in the light of information now available, should share equal blame—temporarily halted moves toward closer Anglo–U.S. defense relations. Indeed, at the height of the affair, the American Sixth Fleet sought physically to obstruct Anglo–French operations in the Mediterranean. But afterwards, each side looked back on what had happened with disquiet.

The British political élite concluded from the disaster that the pursuit of any foreign policy which was not underpinned by American support was unviable. (Part of it also concluded that only through integration with Europe could this dependence be curtailed—something the U.S. was remarkably slow to grasp.) The Americans, for their part, soon recognized the dangers of encouraging a complete withdrawal of Britain from international engagements, even in the Middle East where competition between the two was sharpest. Anti-colonialism would henceforth gradually take second place to anti-communism in U.S. motivations. And so Britain was transformed within the American political psyche from selfish rival to selfless ally—though not without occasional role reversals.

In these circumstances, and under a new British Prime Minister, Harold Macmillan, Anglo–American relations rapidly improved. Even the McMahon Act was finally repealed in 1958 as part of a renewal of nuclear cooperation. It soon bore fruit. Eisenhower and Macmillan agreed on the deployment of 60 Thor missiles equipped with nuclear warheads, provided by the U.S. but under joint U.S.–U.K. control. With the resumption of links, the Americans were also surprised to learn how advanced Britain's own nuclear program was. On this basis of shared interests and contributions, a new framework for nuclear collaboration was built.

But technical and funding difficulties for the nuclear deterrent on both sides of the Atlantic soon prompted a crisis that threatened Britain's fundamental interests. The British Blue Streak missile, intended to carry the country's nuclear weapon, was cancelled on grounds of mounting cost. Eisenhower had previously agreed that it should be replaced by the U.S.-produced, air-launched Skybolt missile. A somewhat vague "gentleman's agreement" was also reached that, in the event of Skybolt's not being suitable, Britain would have the option of purchasing the U.S. Polaris submarine-launched missile.

Skybolt was always the preferred British choice, mainly because it would allow Britain to preserve the life of its V-bomber force, but with the change of Administration, doubts were increasingly voiced about Skybolt's viability. In December 1962, the news broke in Britain that it was to be scrapped. In truth, British Ministers must have known what was in the wind, and they seem to have adopted an attitude of shock partly to put moral pressure on the Americans. Real enough, however, was the wave of anti-American feeling, comparable to that following Suez, which greeted news of this unilateral decision.

At a tense summit in Nassau, Macmillan made it clear to Kennedy that nothing less than the strategic basis of the Special Relationship was at stake if the U.S. did not provide Polaris as a substitute for Skybolt. He warned of the fall of the British government over the issue—Macmillan's political position was indeed shaky at the time—and raised the spectre of an anti-American line being taken by any successor, whether Labour or Conservative.

Kennedy's initial strong reluctance to meet the British request stemmed from advice offered by both the Pentagon and the State Department. There was, in fact, an unspoken desire in Washington to see Britain's nuclear deterrent wither on the vine. This was partly to discourage nuclear proliferation—or, put differently, to ensure an American nuclear monopoly in the West (at least, except for France). There was also a somewhat contradictory desire to entrust any new weapon to a European (or NATO) "Multilateral Force" (MLF), a nebulous conception that survived in the ambiguous wording of the final agreement that was reached.

In the end, through a triumph of personal diplomacy by Macmillan, and through Kennedy's good sense, which exceeded that of his advisers, Britain got Polaris. The done deal was an extremely good one for both sides. Britain obtained a nuclear deterrent with the best available technology and on favorable terms. At the same time, the U.S. cemented its strategic relationship with the U.K., both through the technology itself and through the implied dependence which this necessarily created.[5]

The period between 1946 and 1962–1963 thus provides some instructive lessons in the operation of the Special Relationship—lessons that are still extremely relevant. The first

[5] John Baylis, *Anglo–American Defence Relations 1939–1984: The Special Relationship* (London: Macmillan, 1984), pp. 29–136; Alistair Horne, "The Macmillan Years and Afterwards," in *The "Special Relationship": Anglo–American Relations Since 1945*, ed. W. Roger Louis and Hedley Bull (Oxford: Clarendon Press, 1986), pp. 87–102; C. J. Bartlett, *"The Special Relationship": A Political History of Anglo–American Relations Since 1945* (London: Longman, 1992), pp. 20–100.

concerns divergences of strategic goals. These divergences were real, not imaginary or merely the result of misunderstandings.

A certain element in the American élite still regarded Britain (and its Empire) as a rival, not primarily as an ally. Even when the Soviet threat to Europe demanded a change of view, a degree of hostility, now tinged with contempt at Britain's miserable economic performance, was evident. The view was not merely that (as Dean Acheson undiplomatically observed) Britain had not yet "found a role" and should not depend on any special treatment from the U.S. to find one, but rather that Britain was simply unworthy of any consideration as a power at all.[6] It followed (according to this view) that Britain should not have its own nuclear deterrent, let alone any technology for it supplied by the U.S. American

[6] Acheson's remarks of December 5, 1962, as the Skybolt crisis was breaking could hardly have come at a worse time for Macmillan. The Prime Minister was extremely annoyed. He confided to this diary: "[Acheson] was always a conceited ass, but I don't really think he meant to be offensive," Alistair Horne, *Macmillan* 1957–1986 [Volume II of the Official Biography] (London: Macmillan, 1989), p. 429.

policymakers were accordingly tempted by the prospect of sidelining or ending the Anglo–American Special Relationship in favor of a new relationship with Western Europe as a whole.

Against these tendencies, however, there worked a powerful combination of circumstances. As has been observed, the Soviet challenge was the most important and most obvious. Only Britain was seen by the American military planners as a serious ally in the event of war. Another factor was France, particularly once de Gaulle arrived on the scene in 1958. At the height of the Cuban missile crisis, the general stood firm against the Soviet Union, but he was the loosest of loose cannons at other times. Moreover, France had no intention of abandoning its genuinely independent nuclear weapon or of subordinating its independent foreign policy to an American-led alliance.[7] French obstructionism, then as since, forced America

[7] For de Gaulle's view, see Jean Lacouture, *De Gaulle*, Vol. III: *Le Souverain* (Paris: Editions du Seuil, 1986). The general had, in fact, decided on his veto of Britain's application to join the European Common Market before the U.S.–U.K. deal reached on the Polaris at Nassau.

back to reliance on Britain. Finally, despite the slow rearmament of West Germany from 1950 on, the Germans never looked, at least until reunification at the end of the Cold War, as if they could rival Britain as a useful ally.

Of course, the ups and downs of the Relationship did not depend entirely upon factors as large and immovable as these. Bad diplomacy, in the sense of poor analysis and use of information, was also important at various points. In 1956, Eden should have known that the last thing Eisenhower wanted on the eve of an election was to be forced to come to the aid of a colonial power. Kennedy's advisers, above all Defense Secretary Robert McNamara, should have grasped what cancellation of Skybolt would mean politically for Macmillan.[8]

Case Study #2: Reagan and Thatcher (1981–1988)

The eight years during which Ronald Reagan and Margaret Thatcher led their respective

[8] See Richard E. Neustadt, *Report for JFK: The Skybolt Crisis in Perspective* (Ithaca, N.Y.: Cornell University Press, 1992).

nations is rightly regarded as the period during which the Special Relationship was closest and most effective. Not everyone, then or since, has approved of the results. It is interesting to recall, for example, that Thatcher was portrayed as Reagan's "poodle" in the wake of her defense of the Libyan raid of 1986, much as the same canine comparison was used later to disparage Tony Blair's conduct during the Iraq War.

In the intervening years, there has also been a certain amount of revisionism. Thus, Conservative Party critics of Tony Blair like to emphasize the occasions on which Mrs. Thatcher forcefully disagreed with the President. Such, indeed, there were, but she never forgot which power was the senior partner and moderated her behavior accordingly.

The indisputable point is that the Reagan–Thatcher axis was the most powerful international alliance of its time, and it has much to teach those wishing to place Anglo–American relations on a stable and sustainable footing today.[9]

[9] For a useful general account of the Reagan–Thatcher relationship, see Geoffrey Smith, *Reagan and Thatcher* (London: The Bodley Head, 1990).

There are two reasons why the relationship was so close.

First, the two leaders always liked and increasingly respected each other; and their personal friendship—an overused word in current politics, but not misapplied in this case—meant that frictions could be borne and crises faced much more easily than would otherwise have been the case.

Second, their political characters were, at root, very similar. This was despite the differences of style, working methods, aptitudes, age, and (of course) sex. Both were motivated by the desire to put into action a series of beliefs: They were, in a favorite Thatcher phrase, "conviction politicians," and they largely agreed. They shared a common philosophy of freedom, one which held that government exists for individuals, not *vice versa*; that it is more often a problem than a solution; that low taxes and light regulation are the secret of growth and jobs; that the Western model of liberty is applicable beyond the West; and that the use of force in liberty's defense is always justified and often necessary.

One should add that they also had two fundamental disagreements, which the differing circumstances of their respective nations served to sharpen and which their friendship was useful in softening.

- The first disagreement related to economics, where Thatcher was a devotee of balanced budgets ("good housekeeping") while Reagan believed that tax cuts, even with ballooning deficits, were vital to increase incentives and promote prosperity. In this, despite the success of the Thatcher economic revolution, it is Reagan's priorities which now look correct.
- The second related to deterrence, where Thatcher was determined to keep the nuclear weapon while Reagan was prepared (at least in his more visionary moments) to embrace the goal of a nuclear weapons–free world protected by the global shield offered by the Strategic Defense Initiative (SDI). In this, despite the importance of SDI in persuading the Soviets to abandon the arms race, it is Thatcher's priorities which seem more sensible.

In fact, the sharpest disagreements did not focus on either of these key points, but rather on secondary issues such as U.S. measures against firms participating in the Soviet gas pipeline project, U.S. claims of extraterritoriality in taxation, and most notably the U.S. invasion of Grenada in 1983. Only the last of these is much remembered today.

The resultant bad feeling between London and Washington was the result of sloppy diplomacy by America and a lack of imagination on the part of Britain. If the U.S. had warned the Thatcher government in a timely manner of what was afoot, Mrs. Thatcher's anger would have been silenced, and perhaps her support might even have been forthcoming. If Britain, for its part, had understood that, whatever the Commonwealth implications, America regarded the Caribbean as in its own backyard and would act unilaterally to prevent another mini-Cuba arising there, matters would have been kept in proportion. One should add that, judging events by their consequences (which is not, of course, the only way to judge them), the American action itself proved to be correct.

The two most difficult issues that arose during this period—ones which could have fractured the Special Relationship even under Reagan and Thatcher if mishandled—were (for Britain) the Falklands War of 1982 and (for America) the Libyan raid of 1986. For Britain, the recovery of the Falklands was a matter of fundamental national interest. This is now easy to forget; too close a concentration on geography renders it easier too. At the time, however, it was true. Had Argentina prevailed, Britain would have been humiliated, and its inclination or ability to play a significant international role would simply have collapsed. America would have lost out severely from that. The Thatcher government would probably have fallen, the program of economic reforms would have failed, and British opinion would have turned sharply against the United States. The world today would look different in two very obvious ways.

- Although the Soviet Empire would probably have imploded anyway, the international economic revolution which has swept the world since and which was inspired by "Thatcherism" would have been stillborn.

- As for Britain, the country would now almost certainly be locked into a European megastate hostile to the U.S.

This reflection shows how wrong were the critics of Mrs. Thatcher in Washington who argued for U.S. neutrality on the (real enough) grounds that American interests in South America would otherwise be damaged. The question, as Macmillan stressed to Kennedy though Thatcher never needed to spell out to Reagan, was simply whether the Special Relationship was going to continue or not. It was, therefore, not only the benevolence of Defense Secretary Caspar Weinberger, but also shared national interests which lay behind the U.S. decision to provide vital intelligence and material assistance in the conflict.

The reasoning behind Britain's support for the Libyan raid was similar. Just as the Reagan Administration had doubts about the Falklands campaign, so the Thatcher government was initially unconvinced of the merits of the Libyan plan. Mrs. Thatcher also knew that it would exact a high political cost at a time when her domestic standing was already weakened. Just as no other British Prime Minister would probably have set out to retake the Falklands, so great were the risks, so none other than Margaret Thatcher would probably have given permission for the use of British bases for the attack on Libya. Yet because the gamble paid off—she restored her political fortunes despite the adverse public reaction—Britain would henceforth wield unequalled influence in Washington and, more important still in the world's greatest democracy, enjoy the grateful affection of the American people.

If one stands back further from the crises of the period, it is easier to see that underlying the successes achieved was the same combination of personal good will between like-minded leaders, the practical realities of national interest, and the ever-present danger posed by the armed might and ideology of the Soviet Union. In the single greatest service that the Reagan Administration did for Britain, all three elements were very obviously in play. That service was not, in the end, the support which the U.S. gave for the Falklands campaign: It was the decision to supply on such favorable terms the Trident II (D4) missile. This made perfect strategic sense, given the shared views of the U.S. and the U.K. and the threat posed to both by the Soviets, but it was Reagan personally who ensured that agreement was reached so painlessly and so swiftly.

Similarly, the greatest service that the Thatcher government did for America was not in supporting the Libyan raid: It was by locking Britain unconditionally into a joint strategy with the U.S. of, first, confrontation and then graduated engagement with the USSR. That decision, it is no exaggeration to say, ensured that the long-standing Soviet hopes of splitting the West came to nothing.

Of course, other leaders, such as French President François Mitterrand and German Chancellors Helmut Schmidt and Helmut Kohl, played a role as well, but Britain's international contribution was unique. Margaret Thatcher revived Britain's economy, strengthened Britain's defense, restored Britain's prestige, and placed these achievements wholeheartedly at the disposal of the leader of the free world, Ronald Reagan, in a strategy which in a few short years won the Cold War. That is, ultimately, the measure of the Special Relationship's success during the 1980s.

ooooo 3 ooooo

Tony Blair and the Special Relationship

Blair and Clinton

It is to Tony Blair's credit that on becoming Prime Minister in 1997, when he had many more pressing domestic policy concerns, he put a very high priority on restoring a good relationship with Washington. Such restoration was certainly necessary. The replacement of George H. W. Bush by Bill Clinton in 1993 had ushered in a period of quite bad Anglo–American relations. John Major's closeness to Bush and the British Conservative Party's foolish involvement in an apparent campaign to discredit Clinton ensured that an atmosphere of personal mistrust prevailed.

The weakness of the Major government was also well-understood in Washington: Contempt thus supplemented dislike. But it was the insistence of the British—especially the two British Foreign Secretaries of the period, Douglas Hurd and Malcolm Rifkind—on sticking to a failed policy in the Balkans which led to a serious rift with Washington. Clinton, with support from leading Republicans including Senator Robert Dole, wanted to lift the arms embargo on Bosnia and launch air strikes against the Serbs to prevent further genocide. The British veto of these plans led to what the U.S. ambassador of the day described as "the worst moment in Anglo–American relations since Suez."[1] Eventually, the U.S. insisted. The Croatian and Bosnian armies, supported by the U.S., shifted the balance of power against Serbia sufficiently to allow peace to be restored by the Dayton Agreement of November 1995.

The departure of Major after the Conservative Party's unprecedentedly severe defeat in 1997 thus permitted a new beginning for the Special Relationship. Blair had, in fact, closely

---

[1] Brendan Simms, *Unfinest Hour: Britain and the Destruction of Bosnia* (London: Allen Lane, 2001), p. 114.

studied Clinton's success and sought to emulate it. In the first few years, he was even prepared to be Clinton's junior partner, notably in the President's attempts to establish an international "Third Way," or "New Middle" (*Neue Mitte*) as Germany's Chancellor Gerhard Schröder preferred to term it.

Nothing serious came out of these summits of left-leaning leaders, a fact that also probably helped Blair's standing with Clinton. Face to face with French Prime Minister Lionel Jospin and other European socialists, Clinton and Blair, who were both committed to resisting big-government socialism, were inevitably thrown together. This, in turn, also aborted the temptation that perennially faces America to find some other alternative "special" partner or group of partners in Europe.

In any case, as in the First Gulf War, Britain proved by far the best ally America could find in an international crisis. Blair alone was prepared to collaborate in or even openly support American attempts to force Saddam Hussein into line or to punish the early manifestations of Islamic terrorism. In one instance, Britain actually took the lead in a major foreign policy initiative involving the U.S.: the NATO campaign of 1999 against Serb forces ethnically cleansing Kosovo. Blair was morally right, but he was also lucky that Yugoslav President Slobodan Milošević buckled when he did and withdrew his forces.

The British Prime Minister was lucky in another respect as well. His prominence in the operation irritated Clinton exceedingly and soured relations. But Clinton was now approaching the end of his term, so the fallout for the Special Relationship was insignificant. Indeed, as it turned out, Blair's track record of liberal interventionism would prepare him well for cooperation with George W. Bush in the wake of the Islamist attacks of 9/11.

Yet while the Clinton–Blair years were more practically fruitful than the Bush–Major years that preceded them, they were also notable for the failure to address two issues of profound importance to the countries' strategic relationship. The first of these was the need to decide how far and in what respects national sovereignty should be yielded to international institutions in the light of what some argued was an unstoppable movement toward "globalization." Britain, for example, strongly supported the proposed International Criminal Court, which the U.S. eventually refused to accept. But this was merely the tip of the institutional iceberg of differences in attitude toward the wider question of universal jurisdiction, "global governance," and the role of the United Nations.

The second question concerned Britain's relationship with the European Union. One could argue, of course, that the doubts on this issue were not new, and one would be right, as these pages have already shown; but Blair's resolve to have Britain play a central, perhaps leading role in Europe meant that, for the first time since the fall of Edward Heath in 1974, Washington was suddenly faced with the full strategic implications of its own long-term approach to European integration. Moreover, the now unmistakably federalist thrust of EU policy generally, and the way in which Britain under Blair had shifted its position on military integration with Europe, required proper analysis from Washington. This it never received.

So the new millennium opened with two large but barely acknowledged problems facing the Special Relationship. They are still unresolved.

Blair and Bush

Tony Blair had determined to forge a close relationship with President George W. Bush right from the moment of the latter's election. In this he was not only following the advice of Bill Clinton; he was also pursuing a well-established strategy of "hug them close" (as his advisers described it), much like that which his successful predecessors adopted toward whoever was in the White House.[2] Bill Clinton had been Blair's "friend," as the British Prime Minister declared at the height of Clinton's troubles in February 1998; but Blair's friendships are never exclusive and always flexible, and George W. Bush soon became his best friend too.

In these early days, Blair's considerable charm was much required. It allowed him to finesse his way out of several tricky situations.

---

[2] The phrase also provides the title of the best account of Blair's relations with Presidents Clinton and Bush (until 2003): Peter Riddell, *Hug Them Close: Blair, Clinton, Bush and the "Special Relationship"* (London: Politico's, 2003).

Thus, he persuaded Bush, quite against the actual contents of the EU agreement signed at Nice in December 2000, that European defense plans posed no threat to NATO. This somewhat shaky basis for his relationship with a conservative U.S. President might well have collapsed, however, were it not for al-Qaeda's attacks on New York and Washington.

Tony Blair's response rightly secured him the President's and the American people's gratitude and admiration. He palpably shared their outrage and immediately offered full support in punishing those responsible. He sat in the gallery as the President addressed Congress ten days after the attacks and heard the applause as Bush declared that America had "no truer friend than Great Britain."

It is fair to say that Britain never stood higher in American affections than at that time. British troops subsequently participated in the American-led campaign against the Taliban in Afghanistan despite various grumbles from the British military and foreign policy establishment. The President's "axis of evil" speech again tested Blair's mettle; but once more, despite criticism in the British media and snide remarks from his own Foreign Secretary, Jack Straw, Blair endorsed both the analysis of the danger and the strategy of "pre-emption" which lay behind it.

The period of the buildup to the war in Iraq was still more difficult for the Prime Minister, and it was now that his broader political approach began to founder. It is, indeed, from the consequences of Blair's actions during those months that many of his own and, more significantly, the Anglo-American Relationship's problems flow. It is important to understand why this is so (and just as important for supporters of the Iraq War as for its critics) because the Special Relationship cannot stand a repetition of what transpired. The trouble stemmed from the fact that although Blair appeared to subscribe to the "everything's changed" doctrine adopted by America, in his heart he did not—perhaps could not—do so.

A Bridge Too Far

President Bush had proclaimed in addressing Congress after 9/11: "Every nation, in every region, now has a decision to make. Either you are with us, or you are with the terrorists." But

Blair, for all his zeal in supporting America, did not really see the world in these terms. He was and is the result of a sort of historic compromise between Left and Right. His considerable success in politics has been built upon an instinctive preference for "both…and" rather than "either…or." He is a creature of compromise, even if his bellicose language serves to disguise it. So, despite the clear message from Washington, he continued to regard Britain's supreme international role as that of a "bridge" between the U.S. and Europe.

This did not reflect reality, and so, as often happens when awkward realities are ignored in international affairs, the path of illusion proved the road to ruin. Of course, Blair could argue that Europe was not exactly (in the President's words) "with the terrorists." But most European countries and the governing bureaucracy of the European Union were certainly not "with" America in the sense of accepting American strategic goals in the war against terrorism. They were, indeed, shocked and appalled by the "axis of evil" speech. They did not see any reason to change their approach of putting commercial interests and political rivalry with the United

States above any need to counter Islamic terrorism and the proliferation of weapons of mass destruction (WMD).

Moreover, in this, the Europeans were far from alone. Despite their own problems with Islamic militants, neither China nor Russia would go along with America's analysis in any consistent manner. Blair particularly wanted good relations with Russia, where he had hoped to recreate with Vladimir Putin Mrs. Thatcher's relationship with Mikhail Gorbachev, and he was also keen to cultivate China; Britain had, after all, been at the forefront of those wishing to renew arms sales to the People's Republic. He had, above all, spent his first four years in office proclaiming the need to strengthen the United Nations. How could he reconcile that multilateralist approach with the new unilateralist mood in Washington—a mood fully shared by the American people?

Even more important, because fundamental to Blair's ability to control events at home, was the fact that his whole approach to managing the Labour Party was thrown into doubt. Of course, most Labour MPs, like their electors, had the greatest sympathy with the American people after 9/11, but that did not remove Labour's deep suspicion of American policy. Labour MPs felt that they had already been drawn into too close an embrace of America because of Blair's "friendship" with first Clinton and then Bush.

They had some reason to be suspicious. Partly through guile and partly because he simply preferred that way of doing things, Blair had led them along a foreign policy path that allowed him to be acclaimed as Washington's friend at the expense of concealing his true intentions from his colleagues. Each step had been solemnly proclaimed as the last: acceptance of U.S. plans for ballistic missile defense but not participation in it; action against Afghanistan but not Iraq; then action against Iraq but only with U.N. approval and as part of a wider coalition. But what then? What if there was no such approval, no wider coalition, and outright hostility from Europe?

At this point, the famous "bridge" analogy seems all too appropriate, but more as the subject of a disaster movie and less as a reassuring metaphor. Bridges can tolerate much buffeting by the elements, but they cannot stand when the span they are bridging expands. Tectonic shifts, like that set off by 9/11, cause them to totter and fall.

Yet Blair hung on desperately to his bridge. He defended it by engaging in an extraordinary globe-trotting campaign of diplomacy, first to gain support for attacking Afghanistan and then, and much less successfully, for the war against Iraq. But he also indulged in and encouraged in others a large amount of wishful thinking. The height of this was perhaps his speech at the George H. W. Bush Presidential Library in Texas on April 7, 2002:

> Forget the talk of Anti-Americanism in Europe. Yes, if you call a demonstration, you will get the slogans and the insults. But people know Europe needs America, and I believe America needs Europe too.

This message was grossly misleading. Europe, at least in the Donald Rumsfeldian sense of "Old Europe," was already profoundly anti-American and would become ever more stridently so. For almost another year, the British Prime Minister squandered his capital in Washington in trying to persuade America to wait until it had a clear authorization from the U.N. Security Council to act against Saddam Hussein.

He could have used it otherwise. He might have tried to ensure that better preparation was made for the aftermath of the war. He could have reassured himself that a political strategy for post-war Iraq engaged as much of Washington's attention as the military or diplomatic strategies for fighting the war. He could have done what Thatcher always did with Reagan: ask those tricky practical questions which get overlooked by politicians, generals, and officials as they cope in Washington with the need to justify themselves to each other and to the media. Instead, Britain became furiously involved in intradepartmental squabbles within the Administration whose existence made successful planning more difficult, not less.

Paradoxically, during the same visit on which Blair airily assured Americans that anti-Americanism was no danger, the difference between America's and Britain's justification for war against Iraq had been nakedly exposed. At a joint press conference with the British Premier, President Bush said, apparently without intentional irony: "Maybe I should be a little less direct and be a little more nuanced, and say we support régime change [in Iraq]."

This was, of course, far from nuanced in Blair's eyes. It was embarrassingly frank. He had been warned that a war undertaken for such a purpose was probably illegal. More important, without this legal cover, he would be unlikely to bring the Labour Party, or perhaps even a majority of his Cabinet, to support it.

For Blair, the only sufficient justification for war was Saddam Hussein's continued possession of WMD. One can debate the extent to which Blair and his officials manipulated or glossed the evidence to suggest that Saddam had these weapons and that they posed a serious threat. The fact is that he had to put all his eggs in this one fragile basket. When it was clear that there were no WMD and that the supporting evidence was wrong, his credibility with the British public as a war leader was irrevocably destroyed, and with it his capacity to lead public opinion in support of America.

What Went Wrong

Could matters have been handled differently? The question is of more than academic interest because it goes to the heart of whether the Anglo–American Special Relationship is sustainable—and a relationship that inevitably crumbles when casualties mount is not.

The answer is, or should be, encouraging: It need not have turned out this way. Given the fact that there turned out to be no WMD, there was always bound to be anger among critics of the war in Britain. Given the failure to bring stability to Iraq and arrest the spiral of military and civilian casualties, that criticism was bound to spread further. But it was the sense of having been deceived, directly by Blair and indirectly by America, that caused the approval ratings for the war to plunge. This was avoidable, but probably not by Blair or any other leader of the British Labour Party. Again, it is important for Americans to understand why this is so.

The Conservative Party leader, Michael Howard, came in for some strong criticism and even, it seems, a severe political snub from the White House because of his attacks on Blair over the war. The Tories deserved what they got; opportunists in matters of war and peace always do. But the fact remains that a Conservative Prime Minister would have been better able to deliver America the sustained support of the British public than was Tony Blair. A direct and simple appeal to British national interest in the Atlantic alliance—and thus to supporting America, right or wrong (though preferably and probably right)—could have been made by a right-of-center politician as it was made, in more or less these terms, by John Howard in Australia. By contrast, Blair's and New Labour's liberal idealist and internationalist ideology precluded such an appeal. That is what prompted the Prime Minister to make exaggerated and subsequently discredited claims to the House of Commons.

The enduring lesson for the Special Relationship is stark: Personal good will—even personal courage of the sort Blair displayed during the crisis—is no substitute for getting the arguments right. And unless one can base one's arguments and subsequent explanations and, when necessary, excuses on the sure foundations of national interest, public support will crumble. This it has done, along with Blair's bridge of Euro-Atlanticism.

The brutal reality is that, as he reaches the end of his time in Downing Street, Tony Blair's legacy is a gravely weakened, not strengthened,

Special Relationship. Of course, Blair is still popular in America, and he will be able to put that popularity to good use during lecture tours for years to come. Britain's Prime Minister also has the ear of the world's most powerful leader. Britain even seems, on occasion, to be able to influence American policy.

- The Administration's shift in favor of aid to Africa reflects one of Blair's private obsessions.
- The U.S. has taken a marginally more favorable view of the Palestinians, at least until the election of Hamas, because of British badgering.
- If, very sensibly, the U.S. has refused to sign up to Kyoto or a successor, American public doubts have, not so sensibly, been toned down on climate change.
- America, equally ill-advisedly, allows its policy toward volatile Southeast Europe to be set largely by the British Foreign Office.[3]

---

[3] See my article, "America, The Hague, and Ante

- Above all, American attitudes toward the European project—very foolishly indeed, as will be explained—have become more favorable, in part to make Tony Blair's life more comfortable.

For these ambiguous triumphs, Blair may take a little personal credit; but what they all have in common is that they do not advance British national interest in the slightest degree, and they accordingly cut no ice with British public opinion. Blair has delivered nothing of substance to the country in exchange for sacrifices that have become highly unpopular. For example, Britain gained no preferential treatment when it came to handing out contracts for Iraqi construction over competitor countries that had spent years bankrolling Saddam and had ferociously opposed the war.

It is unfair to describe the U.S. Administration as ungrateful: It has never been asked for any favors worth having. Instead, the inside accounts of Blair's dealings with the President

---

Gotovina: The Railroading of a Former U.S. Ally," *The American Spectator*, March 2006.

have conveyed to the British public a slightly pathetic selflessness, which might be accounted an asset in a personal friend but seems misplaced in a national leader.

Blair's Legacy

The cumulative result of Blair's relationship with Bush is that its very closeness has brought America's standing in Britain low—not so low, it is true, as in most of Europe, let alone in the Muslim world, but lower than it should be and substantially lower than, for example, in India.[4]

- Not only do a large majority of the British now believe that the war in Iraq was wrong, but they also feel that the world is less safe since Saddam went. A poll taken after the hundredth British military death in Iraq showed that 62 per cent favored withdrawal.[5]

---

[4] For this and what follows, see the detailed *16-Nation Pew Global Attitudes Survey* of June 23, 2005.

[5] Populus poll for *The Times* (London), February 8, 2006.

- Even support for the U.S. war against terrorism has dropped since 2002 from almost 70 per cent to barely 50 per cent.
- Overall, the British, like the other main European nations, now support a more distant foreign and security relationship with the U.S. They give higher favorability ratings to Germany, France, Japan, and even China than to the U.S.[6]

Of course, some of this should be taken with several spoonfuls of salt. In most of the world, it is whether a great power is respected (or even feared) that counts more than whether it is liked when determining how other powers behave toward it. The Roman proto-dictator

[6] On the other hand, the British remain more favorable toward the American people than are any other European country; and in a study of various unpleasant characteristics, which might or might not be associated with Americans, the British are more likely than others to think Americans polite and morally upright. This, though, is only moderately encouraging. See *Pew Global Attitudes Survey*, June 23, 2005.

Sulla's favorite epigram—"Let them hate me, as long as they fear me"—contains more wisdom than is often allowed.

That said, being as unpopular as America now is in most Western countries does constitute a serious indirect weakness for American power. It means that, as recently in Germany and Spain and as regularly in France, European politicians play up to anti-Americanism to get elected, and this makes subsequent co-operation with the U.S. much more difficult. This is even more important in Britain, precisely because the Special Relationship has always been based upon strong popular support and because Britain, like America, is a country where democracy is both vibrant and demanding.

Perhaps the greatest damage done to America's reputation over the past few years is within the British liberal establishment: the intelligentsia, the civil service mandarinate, the more powerful media people, and a sprinkle of senior politicians. Within this group, anti-Americanism has always, of course, been rife; but the enemies of the American superpower have been given new heart, and the uncommitted majority are less inclined than in the past to tell them to be quiet. Anti-Americanism is now taking some extreme forms, more reminiscent of the late 1960s or of the height of the Cold War in the early 1980s. Thus, we find the British playwright Harold Pinter using his Nobel Lecture last December to declare:

> The crimes of the United States have been systematic, constant, vicious, remorseless.... I put it to you that the United States is without doubt the greatest show on the road. Brutal, indifferent, scornful and ruthless it may be, but it is also very clever.... It also has its own bleating little lamb tagging behind it on a lead, the pathetic and supine Great Britain.

Hardly great prose, and not obviously rational: but Pinter did get his Nobel Prize. A further, rather more significant example is that of Sir Rodric Braithwaite, former British ambassador in Moscow and at one time chairman, no less, of the Cabinet's Joint Intelligence Committee (JIC):

> Whatever other casualties the Iraq war produces, whatever difficulties appear in the aftermath, one thing is clear. Even in victory the principles on which British foreign policy have been based since Suez are now among the walking wounded.... There is, in any case, a good deal less to the special relationship between Britain and the US than meets the eye. For the British it is an emotional comfort blanket for a declining power.[7]

And so the diatribe continues, concluding, very predictably, with a call for Britain to integrate further with Europe. The political forces seeking to drive a wedge between Britain and America are thus more confident than they have been for many years. Americans should expect this to make Britain a less reliable partner—unless something is done to solve the problems which Tony Blair's term as Prime Minister has contrived to create.

[7] Rodric Braithwaite, "End of the Affair," *Prospect*, May 2003.

ooooo 4 ooooo

Britain and the Special Relationship

THE BRITISH VOICES raised against the Special Relationship may be louder now, but their arguments have not changed, and they are still wrong. Even the analogy with the "bridge," which was at root a timid attempt to make the Anglo–American alliance more acceptable to its detractors, both misconstrues and underrates the benefits which Britain and America gain from the Relationship.

Britain no longer needs, if it ever needed, to be partially integrated into Europe to gain a hearing in Washington. Similarly, the days when Washington needed London as a means of influencing Europe are gone, partly because the Europeans are less important anyway, partly because the European Union is determined to go its own way, and partly because almost the last world leader the other Europeans are inclined to heed is Britain's Prime Minister—this or any other one, incidentally.

Economic Benefits

Britain's gains from its closeness to America are more solid and more clearly identifiable. Perhaps the most obvious two-way benefit is economic: The U.K. and the U.S. are the largest single source of overseas investment in each other's economies. In 2004–2005, U.S. investment in the U.K. rose by 47 per cent, accounting for more than the combined U.S. investment going to Germany, France, the Netherlands, and Ireland.[1] This propensity to trade, despite the protectionist measures erected occasionally by the U.S. and fairly consistently by the EU, bears eloquent testimony to the ease with which Americans and the British do business with onc another.

Trade is facilitated, of course, by a common language (and not obstructed, be it noted, by lack of a common currency). It is also easier because

[1] UK Trade and Investment Agency figures, June 29, 2005.

the U.S. and U.K. business cultures and legal systems are so similar. There is mutual acceptance of the benefits of competition, most obviously manifested in the willingness by regulators to see takeovers, and of the advantages of light regulation. The fact that Britain is so closely connected to the mighty American economy, whose performance continues to outshine that of Europe in every respect—GDP growth, productivity growth, innovation, and job creation—is particularly important for the British standard of living.

That importance reflects another feature of Britain's unique global position: the fact that, of the major world economies, it is the one most dependent on trade. About half of that trade, depending on how it is measured, is with Europe; but the rest of it is with faraway countries of which, although it cannot be said that the British "know little," it must be admitted that they can do rather little to protect their interests.

Here, too, closeness to America is vital to British success. In previous decades, it was the matter of keeping open the sea-lanes that most preoccupied successive British governments anxious to promote the country's commercial prosperity. Certainly, that is still a factor in

Britain's defense profile. But both unhindered access to reasonably priced raw materials and the security of foreign investments rely nowadays on something more than gunboat diplomacy (even if Britain had sufficient gunboats). They have to depend, in the last resort, upon stability underpinned, and if necessary imposed, by the United States.

That is true above all in the Middle East, in West Africa, in Central Asia, and around the Pacific Rim, where without U.S. involvement Western energy supplies could be jeopardized or Western markets imperiled. But it is true globally too, for without the prevailing assumption that America could deal, if necessary, with any power that challenged global order, economic confidence would plummet and the worth of Britain's investments and income along with it. So the British have much for which to thank America—which, when remembered, should help to allay the occasional and inevitable curse.

Intelligence Sharing

In all probability, however, the single most important benefit enjoyed day by day by the citizens of the United Kingdom from Anglo–American collaboration is almost unsung and, necessarily, for the most part unpublicized. This is the privileged position accorded by America to Britain in the sharing of intelligence. It is also the one area where there has been an unbroken line of cooperation. Having begun with the need to penetrate the plans of the Axis Powers, the intelligence services of the two allies soon moved to monitoring the activities of the Warsaw Pact. Today, within a well-established framework, the agencies of the U.K., the U.S., Australia, Canada, and New Zealand continue to share intelligence. U.S. representatives even attend part of the weekly sessions of the JIC.

The precise degree of interchange is, naturally, itself secret, and it certainly varies according to the behavior of the participating powers and the precise nature of threats; but British intelligence continues to enjoy a unique relationship with its U.S. opposite numbers in all matters of vital national interest, especially under present conditions of vigilance against Islamic terrorism. As John Negroponte, the U.S. Director of National Intelligence, recently observed:

"The British have long been our closest counterterrorism partners—the seamless cooperation in the aftermath of the July attacks in London reflected that commitment."[2]

British politicians critical of Britain's closeness to the U.S., and in particular the country's prominent role in Afghanistan, sometimes suggest that terrorist outrages on British streets are the price the nation pays for such involvement.[3] What they do not acknowledge, however, is that the Islamic terrorist threat, which did not begin with the American-led invasion of Iraq and will not end with its ocupation, can be countered only by intelligence and that without U.S. intelligence cooperation, British streets would be still less safe and British citizens at still greater risk.

---

[2] John D. Negroponte, Director of National Intelligence, statement before Committee on Intelligence, U.S. Senate, February 2, 2006, p. 3.

[3] For example, Kenneth Clarke, former Chancellor of the Exchequer and recent Tory leadership candidate, has said: "The decision by the UK Government to become the leading ally of President Bush in the Iraq debacle has made Britain one of the foremost targets for Islamic extremists." Quoted in *The Independent*, September 1, 2005.

Britain's Secret Intelligence Service (MI6) and Security Service (MI5) are highly effective in their special fields of human intelligence acquisition or HUMINT; but in communications intelligence, the United States is far ahead of anyone else. Of course, intelligence information—particularly communications intelligence, which needs to be carefully sifted and analyzed to make sense—is not infallible. If it were, neither the outrage of 9/11 in New York and Washington nor that of the London bombs of July 7, 2005, would have occurred. That, though, is an argument for improved information gathering and more use of HUMINT, not for risking current information sharing, which is what the long-term effect of leaving America to her own devices would inevitably involve for Britain.

Indeed, a useful initiative for any incoming British government to take now would be to re-examine with the United States whether there are not ways in which Britain's HUMINT skills and traditional links with much of the Islamic world, including that part of it which is now resident in Britain itself, could be put to better use. The more that Britain gives to the intelligence relationship the more it can (and should) expect to receive back from it.

Military Strengths and Weaknesses

In the end, Britain's worth to America will always be measured by the country's willingness and ability to deploy effective military power alongside its ally. This cannot be too often or too emphatically stated: Unfortunately, British politicians, including Tony Blair, who privately recognize the fact never put the point so bluntly. It needs to be made, though, because it dispels the illusion that Britain can enjoy security and influence on the cheap.

To this, the obvious rejoinder is to point to the fact that more than a hundred British servicemen have now lost their lives in Iraq. This is a real sacrifice, though it pales before the number of U.S. troops who have died. One could add that no other American ally has committed anything like the military effort that Britain has done. British special services, probably the best in the world, were heavily engaged in the early part of the campaign against the Taliban. In Iraq, the commitment continues. The British control their own zone around the port of

Basra and, despite the serious growth of Iranian and radical Shia influence, continue at least to keep the lid on the cauldron. Several thousand more British troops have recently been sent on a dangerous (and in many ways unsatisfactory) mission in Afghanistan. Britain is pulling its weight.

The trouble is that Britain's weight, in the sense of its overall military capability, is inadequate for the tasks which it faces and which, as America's leading ally, it must expect to continue to face. Like other NATO countries, including the United States, Britain sharply reduced its defense expenditure at the end of the Cold War. Both countries, as almost everyone can now see and some saw at the time as well, cut too far. The U.S. Army was downsized by 30 per cent in the 1990s, which is one reason why the strain of Iraq is so intense; but unlike America, which at least pushed up its spending after the attacks of 2001, Britain has not increased spending at all to cope with the new threats. Indeed, since Tony Blair became Prime Minister in 1997, budgeted defense spending as a share of GDP has fallen from 2.7 percent to about 2.3 percent.

In fact, this understates the problem in three important ways. First, Britain gets less for every dollar spent on defense than does the United States; and this is connected with (though not wholly dependent on) the second problem: that Britain commits less to weapons research. One should add that only Britain and France among European countries have any significant military research and development (R&D) spending at all.

Defense budget percentages on R&D are somewhat misleading, simply because the total sums involved bear no comparison with each other. In 2004, the U.S. spent more than twice as much on defense as the 25 EU member states combined. So when one looks at defense R&D, one finds that the U.S. spends almost exactly ten times as much as the UK.[4] Yet it is precisely through keeping and, where possible, increasing its technological lead that the U.S. is ensuring its unchallenged status of global superpower. And it is because Britain has not either itself invested

---

[4] Burkard Schmitt, "Defence Expenditure," European Union Institute for Security Studies, February 2005.

enough or drawn sufficiently on American expertise that it is becoming questionable whether forces from the two countries will be able to serve together in future years on the same battlefield.

The huge gap between the capabilities of the allies first became embarrassingly clear in the 1999 air operations over Kosovo. Tony Blair was prominent in the martial rhetoric, but the British bombs—when the British aircraft could fly at all—almost always missed their targets. Similarly, in Iraq, the fact that the British were given their own separate zone to run was not just sensible military division of labor: It was an implied reflection of the difficulty of integrating British forces effectively when the Americans had more advanced equipment.[5]

The third problem facing the British armed forces is that while the resources committed have

[5] This at least is the case of "Blue Force Trackers" (a satellite-based tracking and communication system) lent by the U.S. to some British formations, which the latter could not or would not use. See the U.S. study quoted by Richard North, *The Wrong Side of the Hill: The Secret Realignment of UK Defence Policy with the EU* (London: Centre for Policy Studies, 2005), pp. 21–22. For North's important broader thesis, see below.

stayed more or less the same, the duties undertaken have greatly expanded, partly in line with the need to stand by America when almost no other power will do so, but also as Tony Blair's policy of liberal internationalist interventionism—what he calls his "doctrine of international community"—takes effect.[6] British troops are thus currently stationed in Afghanistan, Belize, Bosnia, Cyprus, the Falklands, Germany, Iraq, Kosovo, Kuwait, Oman, Sierra Leone, and, of course, Northern Ireland. In none of these locations have British forces been superfluous. In all, they have been a force for good. The fact remains, however, that today's mismatch between the resources committed to defense and the expanding ambitions of New Labour liberal interventionism cannot continue.

The short-term consequences of this are already apparent. The length of time between tours has been cut: Government guidelines state that deployments should be 24 months apart, but the average for infantry units is now down to 21 months, and for some elements of the Army, it is

---

[6] Tony Blair spelled out the concept at a speech to the Economic Club of Chicago on April 22, 1999.

less than a year. This has a cumulatively bad effect on morale. Not surprisingly, recruitment in all three services has fallen in recent years. The long-run effect is, though, bound to be more serious. The risk is that at some point, despite their professionalism and fighting spirit, British forces may be sent into battle and fail in their mission.

There are two separate issues here. One is that of procurement; but since this fits so closely with the subject of the following chapter—the damaging effects of European integration on Britain's role in the Special Relationship—it can be considered at that point. The other issue is the scale of resources committed by Britain to its defense responsibilities and how that relates to the current plans for reshaping the military.

The British Ministry of Defence is rightly committed to restructuring the country's armed forces so as to take advantage of the so-called Revolution in Military Affairs, combining the use of instantly available networked information and the large-scale use of precision firepower. This involves, for the Army, development of a fully integrated Network Enabled Capability (NEC) and an emphasis on fast, medium-weight vehicles. It also means, in general, fewer platforms, with particular implications for the Navy and Air Force.

An "effects based approach" of the sort the British planners have adopted requires maximum flexibility. The trouble is that it does not, of itself, require fewer personnel; it is certainly not cheaper; and simply because nothing is less predictable than the shape and timing of the next war, one cannot afford capability gaps at any stage. Most important is the fundamental planning assumption which Margaret Thatcher has urged:

> To the question of what precise overall capabilities, and thus exactly what levels of defence spending, are necessary to cope with such scenarios I can only answer: "More than at present—and possibly much more than you think."[7]

This is not happening. The period of transition, therefore, involves worrying risks. If the first military lesson of Afghanistan and Iraq is the importance of technological superiority,

[7] Margaret Thatcher, *Statecraft: Strategies for a Changing World* (London: HarperCollins, 2002), p. 41.

the second is that without sufficient men on the ground, that superiority may prove worthless. Yet all three British services are now facing manpower cuts: 1,500 for the Army, 1,500 for the Navy, and 7,500 for the Air Force.

- The Air Force is also to lose three Jaguar squadrons two years earlier than planned, and the replacement Typhoons will not enter full operational service until the end of the decade.
- The Navy will lose three type 42 destroyers and three type 23 frigates.
- The last of the Sea Harriers is being taken out of service, and the Royal Navy will then have no close air defense until 2015.
- Problems with the Joint Strike Fighter, and particularly the variant needed to replace the Harriers, have also thrown into doubt the future viability of the two new supercarriers for which the Navy budget is being squeezed.

The Navy, it seems, is always—and oddly for a maritime nation—at risk of decimation in the name of one scheme or another. On a previous occasion, planned cuts almost rendered the retaking of the Falklands impossible. As part of the deal to supply Trident II, the Reagan Administration even imposed the condition that cuts in the surface fleet should be reversed.[8]

It was right to intervene in this way, even under a Thatcher government. In the current climate of British politics, where butter can always be guaranteed to win over guns, the U.S. should be much more vigilant about British plans. After all, it is part of the Special Relationship that, *in extremis*, one partner assumes the burdens of the other. The U.S. may suddenly find itself having to take the strain as a result of the U.K.'s imprudence.

[8] Margaret Thatcher, *The Downing Street Years* (London: HarperCollins, 1993), p. 248.

ooooo 5 ooooo

Britain and Europe

IN ASSESSING THE DANGERS to the Special Relationship, it is important to distinguish between the short term, the long term, the avoidable, and the inevitable. Short-term problems will always arise because of marginal clashes of national interest and occasional miscalculations by governments. Some long-term difficulties are inevitable also. America, as a great power, will always be ready in certain conditions to downplay its relations with any single ally in order to see that its global supremacy and security are maintained.

What those who want to make the Special Relationship a success should be keenest to ensure, however, is that there are no long-term, avoidable clashes of fundamental interest between Britain and America. Yet today, as for the past few years, precisely such a disjuncture has been contrived by the approach that

Britain, with significant American encouragement, has taken toward its relations with the European Union.

American Illusions

As noted earlier in these pages, the United States has long pressed Britain to become more involved in mainland Europe. Washington's attitude in recent years has become more equivocal, and skeptical voices have been raised questioning whether this policy any longer made sense. But no alternative approach has ever been seriously suggested, let alone pursued. So the foreign policy bureaucracies in the U.S., the U.K., and the European Union have, as bureaucracies do, carried on working within earlier guidelines and not taken too much notice of what ephemeral politicians think.

It is in the defense sphere, and thus in the Pentagon, that under both the Clinton and Bush Administrations the sharpest questions have been raised about present directions, and rightly so. The U.S. Defense Department and the American military have seen for themselves that the prospectus held out by the Euro-enthusiasts has proved completely false.

This prospectus had two basic elements. The first was that Europe, as a wealthy and populous emerging superpower, had the resources to play a partnership role with the United States in global affairs. The second was that the Europeans could be encouraged to develop the collective will to take up the burden with Britain, as the most Atlanticist European power, playing a crucial part.

As every year goes by, it becomes clearer that Europe is not made for the role of a superpower of even the more modest sort. Europe is a civilization in decline, and it is characterized by dying nations. By 2050, half of Europe's population will be over 50 years old. Support ratios (the ratios of 15–64-year-olds to 65-and-overs) are rapidly worsening. The estimated total fertility rate (the average number of children born per woman over the course of her lifetime) in 2005 in the European Union was 1.5, well below the replacement rate of 2.1.[1] In Germany, most of the new EU members, and—still worse—Italy and Spain, fertility rates have plunged disastrously. Britain and France are the exception, though in

[1] For individual countries, see Appendix 1, "Total Fertility Rates, Europe and America."

these as in other European countries, first- and second-generation immigration fertility brings security and other problems, which may more than compensate for the economic benefits.

Europe's one-time boasts about how the bloc's 450 million–strong population dwarfs that of the U.S. look increasingly hollow as America's population soars. One credible projection has Europe's population in 2050 at 360 million and falling and America's at 550 million and rising.[2] This is a result of both natural increase and immigration—and U.S. immigration is from a Christian culture and thus far more easily assimilated than the predominantly Muslim immigration flooding into Europe. Population size and population growth are important because, other things being equal, countries with large, young populations are better at raising armies, and countries whose populations reproduce often have the self-belief that makes for assertive policies abroad.

European population decline is also linked to the EU's other and even more immediate weakness: relative economic decline. The major

---

[2] "Demography and the West: Half a billion Americans?" *The Economist*, August 22, 2002.

European countries have proved incapable of serious economic reform. Governments which do initiate tentative reforms are thrown out of power; others—like Angela Merkel's Christian Democratic Union–Christian Social Union–Free Democratic Party alliance, which began by proposing tax cuts and now, in a Grand Coalition, proposes tax increases—abandon reform before it has even started.

Europe's businesses are already held back by high taxes, heavy regulation, and restrictive labor laws. The ambitious EU Lisbon economic reform program, devised in that city in 2000, has run into the sand. Europe's productivity growth has fallen over the past decade while America's has risen. Europe's GDP per head is now 25 percent lower than America's, and the gap is widening. It has been estimated that in 20 years, on present trends, the average U.S. citizen will be twice as rich as the average French or German. (Britain is a partial exception and lies somewhere between the two poles).[3] Unemployment

[3] Organisation for Economic Co-operation and Development, *Economic Policy Reforms: Going for Growth*, 2005 edition.

in France and Germany is about twice the level of America's, and Europe's answer is still to reduce the number of hours worked rather than to increase the level of output.

Each upward blip in growth levels, like Germany's recently, is greeted as the first swallow of spring; but summer never comes, and under prevailing conditions and with present attitudes, it never will. For America to bank on Europe's future as a major allied strategic force, as opposed to viewing it as a minor strategic nuisance, is a mistake. For the U.S. to weaken or even abandon the Special Relationship with the U.K. as part of that mistaken approach would be folly—and, given the rate of European integration, an irrevocable folly at that.

If the first assumption—that Europe has the ability be a partner to the U.S.—is flawed, the second—that it will want to—is equally so. The U.S. has persisted in the idea that Europe would be prepared to pay more toward its own defense if, as a *quid pro quo*, the Europeans were given a stronger voice in NATO. Why America ever believed this is unclear. It may result from a difference of political culture. Americans still honor the connection between power and responsibility. Europeans, by and large, do not; they simply want power—in this case, above all, the power to stand up to America.

So there was never the slightest likelihood of European governments' asking European electorates to pay more in taxes for their defense. Nor have they done so.[4]

- Germany, for example, spends about 1 percent of its GDP on defense. Whether Chancellor Merkel changes that will be an interesting measure of any real change of German policy toward the Atlantic Alliance, but America should not bet on it.
- The newer NATO members have inherited from their communist past inefficient conscript armies.
- For their part, Greece and Turkey are more likely to fight each other than they are to fight anyone else; and Turkish opinion is now dangerously

[4] See Appendix 2, "NATO Defense Expenditure by Country as a Percentage of GDP, 2004 (Based on Constant Prices)."

hostile to the U.S., so Turkey can hardly be regarded as a reliable ally at all (something which should perhaps have had an impact before now on American enthusiasm to bring the Turks into the EU).

- France, though a member of NATO and a serious military power, also defines its policies against America rather than otherwise.

The British have not made much of an effort in terms of spending either; but at least they are reliable—a reliability that was always a given fact but is only likely to be lessened, not increased, by further integration into Europe. That, indeed, is why Britain's growing European orientation poses a threat to U.S. interests.

Britain, first under John Major and then, with much greater speed and gusto, under Tony Blair, has been shifting its focus of military cooperation away from the United States and toward the Continent. Outsiders may find that implausible. Did not, after all, Major's government suffer from angry splits on Europe? Has not Tony Blair proclaimed he would stand with

America in its time of trial and even joined in America's wars, and has he not done so against strong opposition from "Old Europe"? Yes, yes, and yes; but the fact remains that the commitments given by British governments ever since Margaret Thatcher left Downing Street, made largely with the approval of U.S. Administrations ever since Ronald Reagan left the White House, have fundamentally altered U.K.–U.S.–European defense relations at the expense of the credibility of NATO and of the future strength of the Anglo–American alliance.

European Military Integration

The NATO Web site proudly boasts that there is a "strategic partnership" between NATO and the EU. There is no such thing, only an incipient strategic competition between America and Europe. The seeds of this were sown first within NATO through misguided emphasis on the so-called two pillars of implicitly equal solidity on each side of the Atlantic and next through elevation of the role of the Western European Union (WEU); but then, as was always predictable, the drive for European military autonomy broke through the framework of

NATO altogether. The EU is, therefore, now a fledging, if feeble, military power with far from feeble ambitions.

Britain once stood out strongly against these developments. Then it started hesitantly to go along with them through the Maastricht Treaty (signed by Major in February 1992), which provided for a Common Foreign and Security Policy, "including the eventual framing of a common defence policy which might lead to a common defence."

Finally, under Tony Blair, who was anxious to prove his European credentials when he started to recognize that he could never bring Britain to accept the euro in place of the pound sterling, the British sought to take the lead. This was always full of danger for Atlanticism for the simple reason that it involved joining in a partnership with France—the only other serious military power in Europe but also the most anti-Atlanticist European state. The deal was done by Tony Blair and President Jacques Chirac in St. Malo in December 1998. The communiqué bluntly stated that the EU "must have the capacity for autonomous action, backed up by credible military forces, the means to decide to use them, and a readiness to do so, in order to respond to international crises." The Clinton Administration was taken by surprise and voiced disquiet, but it was too late.

All the rest has flowed from the St. Malo agreement. The "rest," as regards America, has focused on the detailed arrangements known as "Berlin plus," which made NATO assets available to the EU (the Europeans having nothing very much of their own at that stage, particularly as regards intelligence, command and control systems, heavy lift, and smart weaponry).

The Europeans, for their part, went ahead with creating the institutions for a separate defense—in effect, if not name, a European army. They set up separate military structures, a Political and Security Committee, a Military Committee, and a Military Staff. They also set themselves the goal of creating a Rapid Reaction Force of some 60,000 armed personnel. Since then, peacekeeping forces under formal EU command have operated in Macedonia and Bosnia, though these have, in truth, been exercises in nomenclature, being NATO responsibilities devolved to the organization's main European elements.

The ultimate proof that the thrust of military thinking in European capitals has nothing to do with supporting America's various global responsibilities is the way in which disagreements with America provide the main impulse for further European defense integration. The most obvious example occurred under the shadow of the Iraq War in April 2003, when—snubbing not just the U.S., but also, and even more deliberately, Britain and Tony Blair—the leaders of France, Germany, Belgium, and that other formidable military power, Luxembourg, met to declare that they would set up a joint military command, a separate headquarters, a special rapid reaction force, a European armaments agency, and a European defense college.

In Europe, integration—or megastate-building as it is more realistically described—proceeds along well-planned lines, but it does so at different speeds and always opportunistically according to times and circumstances. From the first, Tony Blair has wanted Britain to be inside this project. Having been thwarted on the euro, he was soon enthusiastic about military integration, but his highest hopes were contained in the project for a European Constitution. This would have brought together all the different elements in a single framework; it would have created a new legal order; it would have set up what constitutions, including the Constitution of the United States of America, always exist to set up: a giant new state—in this case, one called the European Union.

In fact, this grand plan had to be abandoned because of popular resentment against centralization, inflexibility, and one-size-fits-all policies (with a fair bit of xenophobia and protectionism thrown in). But that decision owes nothing at all to any messages coming out of America. The attitude of the Bush Administration toward the project was indeed astonishing and suggests both remarkably little understanding of what is at stake in Europe and a very weak grasp of what developments there mean for the U.K.–U.S. Special Relationship.

Thus, immediately after his re-election, President Bush—pressed by his advisers to try to patch up strains with Europe as if these were the result of a few minor misunderstandings rather than a gaping disagreement about ends and means—spoke warmly of the plans for further integration, though stopping just short of endorsing the European Constitution. Secretary of State Condoleezza Rice went further. She told the London-based *Financial Times*:

> As Europe unifies further and has a common foreign policy—I understand what is going to happen with the Constitution and that there will be unification, in effect, under a foreign minister—I think that also will be a very good development. We have to keep reminding everybody that there is not any conflict between a European identity and a transatlantic identity.[5]

The Constitution as a project is dead, but anti-EU sentiment has not been translated into any new sympathy for Atlanticism. In any case, various elements of the Constitution are being revived and are even coming into effect, though without the irritating unpredictability of democratic involvement.[6] Perhaps the single most

[5] Interview with *Financial Times*, February 11, 2005.

[6] For example, despite the failure of the Constitution project, the EU is setting up a diplomatic corps

important element for the Special Relationship, however—one which has continued altogether unchecked—is the progress of European defense procurement policy.[7]

Defense Procurement Issues

Defense procurement is, in fact, an ideal means of securing European integration, because changes of direction occur largely unnoticed; because once these changes have been made, they are difficult to unravel; and because lead times in weapons development are so long. But now is a particularly sensitive moment because of the technical revolution in warfare to which British and European forces are having to adapt. The cost and complexity are immense:

(the External Action Service) and a European Public Prosecutor's Office; is implementing its Charter of Fundamental Rights; and has established an External Borders Agency, a Human Rights Agency, an Arms Procurement Agency, a Space Programme, and other institutions foreseen by the draft Constitution.

[7] For what follows, see Richard North, *The Wrong Side of the Hill: The Secret Realignment of UK Defence Policy with the EU* (London: Centre for Policy Studies, 2005), which provides copious evidence of the new procurement approach.

the use of satellites, electronics, new land vehicles, unmanned aircraft, and weapons systems are involved. Coming up with the best solutions is hard enough, but ensuring that these result in systems compatible with one's allies so that forces can fight alongside one another is no less important.

Moreover, beneath the pragmatic decision-making lies the reality that not just in industrial, but increasingly in political (and potentially in military) terms, Europe and America are in competition. In recent years, there have been clear signs that as a result of a combination of British government policy, the operation of European institutions, and, on occasion, a lack of imagination by America, Britain is moving away from partnership with the U.S. toward dependence on the EU. This has grave implications for the U.K.–U.S. Special Relationship, which—as Churchill recognized—must be a military partnership or it is nothing.

The British Ministry of Defence now prefers to purchase equipment supplied by companies based in France, Germany, Italy, and Sweden. British troops will be carried to their destinations by European, not American, aircraft. When there, they will use European-constructed battle reconnaissance vehicles and unmanned air vehicles to gather intelligence about enemy movements. They will use European-made howitzers. They will receive logistical supplies transported in European trucks. The European Defence Agency, which began work in January 2005, is setting its own standards, which may well soon come to conflict with those of NATO.

The key to the whole future divergence, however, is the EU's Galileo satellite positioning and communication system, which has been devised as a rival to the U.S. Navstar. The proposed European Rapid Reaction Force, of which Britain is due to provide a central element, is to use Galileo. Questions of technical incompatibility can, it is true, almost always be overcome, and it is important not to suggest that divergences of standards and systems will of *themselves* preclude collaboration by American and British forces. But in this case, the technical differences *themselves* reflect political differences and are, indeed, the fruit of them. They are thus doubly significant.

The Pentagon, which has the strongest interest in keeping Britain alongside, has done little so far to counteract the procurement pressures from Europe. The way in which decisions have been made—or appear to have been made—about the Joint Strike Fighter (JSF), where Britain is the only Tier One foreign partner, is a case in point. Britain was relying on a variant of this aircraft, the F-35B, to defend its two supercarriers, but the F-35B is apparently to be cancelled. Suddenly, it looks as if a European alternative may be required instead.

The affair is a classic example of the harm that can be done by failing to reflect upon the wider implications of U.S. procurement policy. There are also what currently seem to be insuperable problems in gaining access to the software codes for the JSF. These are vital to allow Britain to maintain and alter the aircraft's capabilities to suit its future needs.

Such clashes on what may at first sight seem technical and commercial matters can have serious strategic consequences. One Skybolt should have been enough. A new approach to collaboration in defense procurement, authorized at the highest level in both the U.S. and the U.K., will be necessary if such problems are not to recur. But this is only one of a number of changes required to keep the Special Relationship strong and effective in the years to come.

ooooo 6 ooooo

Securing the Future

THE CONTENTION OF THIS BOOK is that the Anglo–American Special Relationship makes sense. It brings benefits to both parties that no other arrangement with different powers could provide. No foreseeable changes—economic, social, or military—need call the Relationship into question as long as both parties nurture it and avoid entanglements that threaten it.

The three most important questions for the future, therefore, are: What can be done to rectify deficiencies exposed in recent years? What elements need to be strengthened? What new features should be created?

These three questions, in turn, can usefully be examined in the light of two more: What can the U.S. bring to the Relationship to make it more useful for Britain? What more can Britain contribute to help the United States?

American Action

America is and will remain the senior partner. Indeed, it is so much the senior partner that the notion of partnership does not entirely reflect reality. It follows from the fact that America is so powerful that it does not need to alter very much its accustomed ways of behavior, and needs to make at most only quite small sacrifices, in order significantly to enhance Britain's position. The most obvious change would be to ensure that British governments, and thus British public opinion, are not taken entirely by surprise by unwelcome U.S. decisions.

In the end, what makes the Special Relationship special is trust. Trust does not guarantee that interests will never diverge or opinions differ, but it is the essential quality in continued cooperation—for example, in matters of intelligence. Britain should be trusted in other matters too, not just defense procurement (about which sufficient has been said), but also in the formulation of U.S. policy toward regions where it may at some time need British assistance. Britain cannot, of course, be allowed a veto; but British views, suggestions, and even objections should be taken seriously and in a more systematic fashion than through personal interventions by the U.K. Prime Minister, let alone through formal diplomatic representations.

For this to happen, however, America needs to establish clearly what it expects from the Special Relationship and how that arrangement should function in the service of U.S. global interests. No such clarity at present exists. Britain is essentially treated as an ally in wartime but just one of the other European powers when, as occasionally happens, peace breaks out. U.S. policy needs to grasp the fact that Britain is not, in any sense that matters, part of Europe, but rather a distinct entity with which the U.S. has a separate relationship that needs to be conducted according to separate rules.

This does not, of course, preclude the U.S. from having other one-to-one relationships with other powers, even other European ones. Heritage Foundation scholars have sensibly urged on the Bush Administration the need to adopt a pragmatic approach toward individual European states rather than try to do business with them through EU institutions.[1] This

[1] See, for example, John C. Hulsman and Nile

would allow the U.S. to take advantage, for example, of Angela Merkel's genuine warmth toward America, in contrast to her predecessor's hostility. It would also allow the U.S. to achieve at least a private understanding with the French government on a range of interests, France being the most independent-minded of the EU countries, except for Britain.

The trouble is that progressive institutional integration in Europe will make all this more difficult. That is another reason, over and above the requirements of the U.K.–U.S. Special Relationship, for the U.S. to reverse its traditional posture and actively seek to discourage the formation of the European megastate—though the damage has largely been done.

The United States should also rethink its systematic approach to dealings with the British government of the day. It needs to rely less on personalities and to concern itself more with trends, structures, interests, and opinion. The weakness of a Special Relationship based on

---

Gardiner, "After Schroeder: U.S.–German Relations in the Merkel Era," Heritage Foundation *Backgrounder* No. 1907, January 11, 2006.

what passes for "friendship" between leaders has already been described, and it is well exemplified by the Bush–Blair contacts. Too much faith is placed in individuals, and too little attention is paid to whether other factors are in place to strengthen the alliance.

The U.S. needs to be more intelligently assertive. It should be keener to put a British Prime Minister on the spot if Britain has failed to pull its weight or has worked against American interests in some other forum. It should spell out exactly what resources it thinks should be committed to Britain's defenses if the British are to serve alongside America effectively.

The U.S. also needs to be much more critical than it has been of Britain's failure to clamp down on Islamic extremism within its borders. London has become derided as "Londonistan" and has retained that dubious distinction long after the French, so often (and rightly) in receipt of American brickbats, have cleared Paris of troublemakers and put in place arrangements to remove any new arrivals who might pose a danger. It has even been estimated that perhaps as many British citizens were fighting on the side of the Taliban as were fighting on the side of the Allies in Afghanistan. This signifies a deep social and cultural sickness. Neither the government nor the Conservative opposition has yet been seriously confronted by the U.S. with the overwhelming need to make Britain a redoubt against terrorism rather than a platform for it.

Similarly, the U.S. is too reticent about the broader trends which threaten the Special Relationship. This is partly because Americans do not want to be seen to interfere—though backhanded interventions do sometimes occur at election time—and partly because they take Britain for granted, albeit in the nicest possible way.

Britain is changing. The country has, since the 1980s, stood part way between the American and European economic models; but under Tony Blair, public expenditure, tax levels, and regulation have combined to shift Britain further away from the system of capitalism practiced with such success in the United States. Ironically, this is occurring at the same time as other European countries—notably those of Central–Eastern Europe, but also even France and Germany, which are cutting back on spending growth—are doing the opposite. The long-term effect of high spending, high taxes, and high regulation is to encourage protection, because businesses become less competitive. From being a force for open markets, Britain thus risks in the longer term being transformed into a force for trade hostility, which will sharpen political hostility, toward the U.S.

More subtle, but arguably even more important, is a divergence of values that is increasingly evident between British and American society. Of course, it does not do to oversimplify. There is not one single British society any more than there is a single American society. Culture wars exist on both sides of the Atlantic, though they are fought more openly—and by conservatives more successfully—in America. Beneath the surface of Britain there is a substratum of conservative values which would be recognizable to any American conservative, though these values are less connected than in the U.S. to religious belief.[2]

The fact remains, however, that Britain has become more socially liberal and less (in the

[2] See the data assembled in Iain Duncan Smith, "Britain's Conservative Majority," Centre for Social Justice, London, December 2004.

classical sense) economically so, while America has been moving in completely the other direction. At one level, this does not matter much. People who share other things in common—language, history, legal traditions, practical interests—can get along well enough even if they live their lives according to very different standards. But at another level, it does matter because, in the end, there can arise such a level of incomprehension about how the other nation views the world that it erodes basic trust in every sphere.

To deal with this, to put across the reasoning behind its policies, and to counter the shocking degree of anti-American bias in the British (primarily electronic) media, the United States needs a far more effective public diplomacy than it has hitherto mustered. At present, such efforts as there are seem to be focused primarily on the Muslim world where, it must be said, the chances of changing minds, let alone winning hearts, are fairly minimal. Meanwhile, the U.S. is in more danger of losing the minds and hearts of the British than it realizes, which in the long run could be even more significant.

Not since the discrediting of the Congress for Cultural Freedom and the demise of the once-glittering *Encounter* magazine has the U.S. really been prepared to act in any decisive manner to shore up support among opinion formers in Western Europe. With mainland Europe largely lost to visceral anti-Americanism, it is high time for a convinced and convincing campaign to rally support for America's mission and values in Britain. It is also time for a more aggressive campaign to counter the poison of anti-American disinformation which so quickly enters the bloodstream of British public opinion.[3]

British Action

This links in with the question of what more Britain can contribute to America so as to strengthen the Relationship. The most important qualities that any British Prime Minister should bring to the Anglo–American alliance today are honesty and frankness. The Administration needs to understand that, although

[3] Huge harm was done to America, for instance, by the BBC's reporting of reactions to Hurricane Katrina. The Prime Minister rightly described this to Rupert Murdoch as "full of hate of America," as Mr. Murdoch subsequently revealed last September.

Britain recognizes the great benefits it derives from closeness to America, Britain is a country with its own fundamental interests, and these will always come first. Britain will make sacrifices, but Britain has the right to expect rewards for them—solid and material gains, as well as gains quantified in the more general terms of influence and standing. But the Administration should always be able to take what the British government says, and above all what the Prime Minister says, at face value.

The price Britain must be prepared to pay for its Special Relationship with the U.S. is that some relationships with other powers, or with international bodies, will be more difficult and on occasion openly hostile. Britain must, therefore, choose between loyalty to America and integration with Europe; and it would, of course, be helpful if America openly recognized this fact as well. At the same time, the British government should stop trying to win points on matters where it thinks it can tweak America's tail without provoking America's wrath—a strategy close to the heart of the Foreign Office and one which explains in large part Britain's attachment to the cause of universal internal jurisdiction and the International Criminal Court, its embrace of the Kyoto approach to climate change, and its vocal if somewhat ineffective involvement in African development issues.

The British government must face up to reality in two other ways that have already been mentioned. It has to recognize that foreign policy, like charity, begins at home and that this applies to British participation in the war against terrorism. Without internal security, no war can be successfully prosecuted, particularly a war against terrorists.

After the attacks of 9/11, it was Britain that drafted U.N. Security Council Resolution 1373, which called on all governments to deny safe haven to terrorists. Yet offering such haven to Islamic extremists is precisely what the Major and Blair governments have consciously done for years.[4] The policy was based on the advice of

[4] This policy, well-known by hearsay, was embarrassingly exposed when it was recently learned that the London-based Islamist preacher Abu Hamza al-Masri, since sentenced on terrorist offenses to seven years in prison and wanted by America, was known as long ago as 1998 to have been connected to terrorist

British police and intelligence services, which mistakenly believed that the Islamists had only non-British targets in their sights. Britain's adherence to the European Convention on Human Rights and, more particularly, the provisions of its own recent Human Rights Act still prevents the speedy expulsion, extradition, or incarceration of Islamist extremists. The British political class has yet to wake up to the fact that this must change if more terrorist outrages in Britain are to be avoided.

So, too, the British government should be much more honest and realistic about the defense budget, which has to be increased to meet not just the requirements of adaptation, but also present and future dangers. There is a further, even less palatable truth which must be digested: Precisely because America has such superiority in defense technology and will therefore become more risk-averse as regards personnel, it will look increasingly to Britain to provide troops. The British government will

---

kidnapping and murder in Yemen, but no action was taken by the authorities. See *The Times* (London), February 9, 2006.

need to prepare public opinion—and this also highlights the need for far better U.S. public diplomacy—for continuing British military casualties in future wars that are themselves an inevitable consequence, as the "axis of evil" speech argued, of the threats which continue to confront the West.

Harold Macmillan, in that irritating way of his, used to suggest that the British were the equivalent of the smooth and enlightened Greeks to America's tough and belligerent Romans; but in any apt comparison for the future, the British must expect to play the role not of sophisticated Athens but of martial Sparta. It is at least true to national character. British youth still loves to fight; it is the traditional accompaniment to popular competitive sport, which the British love almost, though not quite, as much. Britain will need substantially to expand its military budget, but British soldiers, who still represent for most British people the archetypical and admirable expression of the British character, will do the rest. This may seem brutal, but it is the bottom line of what Britain brings, and can continue to bring, to its otherwise unequal relationship with the American superpower.

There is, though, another series of engagements on a different plane that also need to be fought. Those British friends of America who are privileged to have a public voice need, quite simply, to speak up in support of some unfashionable truths. They should, for example, point out that it is Europe and, in some respects, Britain that are dysfunctional, not the United States.

- When the British liberal media laugh at American religiosity, the friends of America might intimate that a sound and simple Christian faith is not an obviously bad background against which to bring up children rather than, as happens frequently in Britain, outside wedlock and with multiple partners.[5]
- They could suggest that a country like the United States which commands the fierce support of its newest immigrants may be healthier and have a

[5] On present trends, half of all British babies will be born outside of wedlock by 2012. Only 35 per cent of children born in a cohabiting union will live with both parents throughout their childhoods. See *Daily Telegraph* (London), February 21, 2006.

sounder view of citizenship than one whose obsession with multiculturalism has turned young British Muslims into suicide bombers who hate the place of their birth.

- Finally, they might tactfully note that America is synonymous with success: the country whose economic performance, cultural tastes, military power, and democratic model have, in open competition, swept aside every alternative before them.

Of course, it would all be easier if the British could then be persuaded to feel—as Margaret Thatcher feels—that they somehow have a "share in America," that they are associated with America's fortunes for good and ill, and that by some mysterious process this makes them more, not less, British.[6] If and when they do feel this, it will truly be possible to say that the Special Relationship is secure.

---

[6] Margaret Thatcher, *Statecraft: Strategies for a Changing World* (London: HarperCollins, 2002), p. 20.

Appendix I
Total Fertility Rates, Europe and America

Austria	1.3 (2001)
Belgium	1.5 (1995)
Bulgaria	1.2 (2001)
Cyprus	1.6 (2000)
Czech Republic	1.1 (2001)
Denmark	1.7 (2001)
Estonia	1.3 (2001)
Finland	1.7 (2001)
France	1.8 (1999)
Germany	1.4 (2000)
Greece	1.3 (1999)
Hungary	1.3 (2001)
Iceland	2.1 (2000)
Ireland	2.0 (2001)
Italy	1.2 (2000)
Latvia	1.2 (2001)
Lithuania	1.3 (2001)
Luxembourg	1.7 (2001)
Malta	1.5 (2001)
Netherlands	1.7 (2001)
Norway	1.8 (2001)
Poland	1.3 (2001)
Portugal	1.5 (2001)
Romania	1.3 (2000)

continued on next page

Appendix 1: Total Fertility Rates, Europe and America (continued from previous page)

Slovakia	1.2 (2001)
Spain	1.2 (2000)
Sweden	1.6 (2001)
Switzerland	1.4 (2001)
Turkey	2.5 (2000)
United Kingdom	1.6 (2000)
United States	2.1 (2000)

Source: United Nations, Department of Economic and Social Affairs, Population Division, *World Fertility Report 2003* (New York: United Nations, 2004).

Appendix 2
NATO Defense Expenditure by Country as a Percentage of GDP, 2004 (Based on Constant Prices)

Belgium	1.3
Bulgaria	2.4
Canada	1.2
Czech Republic	1.9
Denmark	1.4
Estonia	1.6
France	2.6
Germany	1.4
Greece	2.9
Hungary	1.5
Italy	1.8
Latvia	1.3
Lithuania	1.5
Luxembourg	0.7
Netherlands	1.6
Norway	1.9
Poland	1.9
Portugal	1.7
Romania	2.1
Slovakia	1.8
Slovenia	1.5
Spain	1.3
Turkey	3.1

continued on next page

Appendix 2: NATO Defense Expenditure by Country as a Percentage of GDP, 2004 (Based on Constant Prices) (continued from previous page)

United Kingdom	2.3
United States	3.8

Source: *NATO–Russia Compendium of Financial and Economic Data Relating to Defence*, compiled by Data Analysis Section, Force Planning Directorate, Defence Policy and Planning Division, NATO International Staff, December 2005, p. 7.